LINCOLNSHIRE

A GENEALOGICAL BIBLIOGRAPHY

by

Stuart A. Raymond

Published by
Federation of Family History Societies (Publications) Ltd,
The Benson Room, Birmingham & Midland Institute,
Margaret Street, Birmingham, B3 3BS, England

Copies also obtainable from:
S.A. & M.J. Raymond, 6, Russet Avenue, Exeter, EX1 3QB, U.K.

First published 1995

Cataloguing in publication data:

Raymond, Stuart A., 1945-
Lincolnshire: a genealogical bibliography. British genealogical
bibliographies. Birmingham, England: Federation of Family History
Societies, 1994.

DDC 016.94253

ISBN: 1-86006-001-3

ISSN: 1033-2065

Printed and bound by Oxuniprint, Walton Street, Oxford OX2 6DP

Contents

Introduction

This bibliography is intended primarily for genealogists. It is, however, hoped that it will also prove useful to historians, librarians, archivists, research students, and anyone else interested in the history of Lincolnshire. It is intended to be used in conjunction with my *English genealogy: an introductory bibliography,* and the other volumes in the *British genealogical bibliographies* series. A full list of these volumes appears on the back cover. The area covered is the historic county of Lincolnshire, as it existed prior to local government reorganisation in 1974. It thus includes South Humberside.

Many genealogists, when they begin their research, do not realise just how much information has been published, and is readily available in printed form. Not infrequently, they head straight for the archives, rather than checking printed sources first. In so doing, they waste much time, and also impose needless wear and tear on irreplaceable archives. However, when faced with the vast array of tomes possessed by major reference libraries, it is difficult to know where to begin without guidance. This bibliography is intended to point you in the right direction. My aim has been to list everything relating to Lincolnshire that has been published and is likely to be of use to genealogists. In general, I have not included works which are national in scope but which have local content. Many such works may be identified in *English genealogy: an introductory bibliography,* to which reference is made at appropriate points below. I have also excluded the numerous notes and queries found in family history society and similar journals, except where the content is of importance. Where I have included such notes, replies to them are cited in the form 'see also', with no reference to the names of respondents. Local and church histories have been excluded except in a few cases. They frequently provide invaluable information for the genealogist, but are far too numerous to be listed here. This is a bibliography of published works; hence the many manuscript histories, transcripts, *etc.,* to be found in Lincolnshire libraries are excluded.

Be warned: just because information has been published, it does not necessarily follow that it is accurate. I have not made any judgement on the accuracy of most works listed: that is up to you. If you are able, it is always best to check printed sources against their originals, to determine how accurate the editor was.

Anyone who tries to compile a totally comprehensive bibliography of Lincolnshire is likely to fall short of his aim. The task is almost impossible, especially if the endeavour is made by one person. That does not, however, mean that the attempt should not be made. Usefulness, rather than comprehensiveness, has been my prime aim — and this book will not be useful to anyone if its publication were to be prevented by a vain attempt to ensure total comprehensiveness. I am well aware that there are likely to be omissions — although none, I hope, of books which every Lincolnshire genealogist should examine. My purpose has been to enable you to identify works which are mostly readily available, and which can be borrowed via the inter-library loan network irrespective of whether you live in London or Melbourne. Most public libraries are able to tap into this network; your local library should be able to borrow most items I have listed, even if it has to go overseas to obtain them.

If you are an assiduous researcher, you may well come across items I have missed. If you do, please let me know, so that they can be included in the next edition.

The work of compiling this bibliography has depended heavily on the resources of the libraries I have used. These included Lincolnshire Local Studies Library, Lincolnshire Archives Office, Exeter University Library, Exeter City Library, the British Library, and the Society of Genealogists, amongst others. I am grateful to the librarians of all these institutions for their help. I am grateful too for the assistance rendered by Lincolnshire Family History Society. Brian Christmas and Eleanor Nannestad both kindly read and commented on early drafts of my manuscript, Terry Humphries typed the manuscript, and Bob Boyd saw the book through the press. I am grateful too to the officers of the Federation of Family History Societies, whose support is vital for the continuation of this series. My thanks also to my wife Marjorie and to my children, who have lived with this book for many months.

Stuart A. Raymond

Abbreviations

A.A.S.R.P.	*Reports and papers of the Associated Architectural Societies*
F.N.Q.	*Fenland notes and queries*
L.A.A.S.R.P.	*Lincolnshire Architectural and Archaeological Society reports and papers*
L.F.H.S.	Lincolnshire Family History Society
L.F.H.S.M.	*Lincolnshire Family History Society [magazine]*
L.H.	*Lincolnshire historian*
L.H.A.	*Lincolnshire history and archaeology*
L.M.I.S.	Lincolnshire marriage index series
L.N.Q.	*Lincolnshire notes and queries*
L.P.P.	*Lincolnshire past and present*
L.P.R.M.	*Lincolnshire parish registers: marriages*
L.R.S.	Lincoln Record Society
L.R.S., P.R.S.	Lincoln Record Society. Parish Register Section
M.G.H.	*Miscellanea genealogica et heraldica*
M.I.L.	Marriage index of Lincolnshire
N.G.	*Northern genealogist*
N.S.	New series
P.P.R.S.	Phillimore's parish register series
S.L.H.A.	Society for Lincolnshire History and Archaeology
S.L.H.A.F.H.S.N.	*Society for Lincolnshire History and Archaeology Family History Section newsletter*

Bibliographic Presentation

Authors' names are in SMALL CAPITALS. Book and journal titles are in *italics*. Articles appearing in journals, and material such as parish register transcripts, forming only part of books are in inverted commas and textface type. Volume numbers are in **bold** and the individual number of the journal may be shown in parentheses. These are normally followed by the place of publication (except where this is London, which is omitted), the name of the publisher and the date of publication. In the case of articles, further figures indicate page numbers.

6

1. THE HISTORY OF LINCOLNSHIRE

There are innumerable books on the history of Lincolnshire. They describe the setting within which our ancestors lived, worked, ate, worshipped and slept, and are therefore essential reading for anyone who wants to understand the world of parish registers and monumental inscriptions. Two good introductions to Lincolnshire history are provided by:

ROGERS, A. *A history of Lincolnshire ...* 2nd ed. Chichester: Phillimore, 1985.

BREARS, CHARLES. *A short history of Lincolnshire.* A. Brown & Sons, 1927.

The authoritative works in the *History of Lincolnshire* series all deserve attention. Those of general interest to genealogists include:

PLATTS, GRAHAM. *Land and people in medieval Lincolnshire.* History of Lincolnshire 4. Lincoln: History of Lincolnshire Committee, 1985.

OWEN, DOROTHY M. *Church and society in medieval Lincolnshire.* History of Lincolnshire 5. Lincoln: Lincolnshire Local History Society, 1971.

HODGETT, GERALD A.J. *Tudor Lincolnshire.* History of Lincolnshire 6. Lincoln: History of Lincolnshire Committee, 1975.

HOLMES, CLIVE. *Seventeenth century Lincolnshire.* History of Lincolnshire 7. Lincoln: History of Lincolnshire Committee, 1980.

BEASTALL, T.W. *The agricultural revolution in Lincolnshire.* History of Lincolnshire 8. Lincoln: S.L.H.A., 1978.

OLNEY, R.J. *Rural society and county government in nineteenth-century Lincolnshire.* History of Lincolnshire 10. S.L.H.A., 1979.

WRIGHT, NEIL R. *Lincolnshire towns and industry, 1700-1914.* History of Lincolnshire 11. Lincoln: History of Lincolnshire Committee, 1982.

MILLS, DENNIS R., ed. *Twentieth century Lincolnshire.* History of Lincolnshire 12. Lincoln: History of Lincolnshire Committee, 1989.

Another authoritative work is the *Victoria County History:*

PAGE, WILLIAM, ed. *The Victoria history of the County of Lincoln.* Archibald Constable & Co., 1906. v.2. Ecclesiastical, political, and educational history, *etc.* No more published.

For an interesting collection of essays, see:

TYSZKA, DINAH, MILLER, KEITH, & BRYANT, GEOFFREY F., eds. *Land, people and landscapes: essays on the history of the Lincolnshire region, written in honour of Rex C. Russell.* Lincoln: Lincolnshire Books, 1991.

See also:

DEAR, JAMES, & TAYLOR, TOM. *Aspects of Yellowbelly history: the settlement and development of the East, West, and Wildmore Fens: a history of the Fens north of Boston.* Spalding: Chameleon International, 1988.

The standard work on the county's architecture is:

PEVSNER, NIKOLAUS, & HARRIS, JOHN. *Lincolnshire.* 2nd ed. The buildings of England series. Penguin, 1989.

Older antiquarian works often contain much more information of genealogical interest than modern histories. See, for example:

ALLEN, THOMAS. *The history of the county of Lincoln from the earliest period to the present time.* 2 vols. Lincoln: John Saunders, 1833-4. Includes a survey of the County.

HALL, JOHN GEORGE. *Notices of Lincolnshire, being an historical and topographical account of some villages in the Division of Lindsey.* Hull: Eastern Morning News, 1890. Parochial survey.

MARRAT, WILLIAM. *A history of Lincolnshire, topographical, historical and descriptive.* 3 vols. Boston: The author, 1814-16. Includes a parochial survey, with some monumental inscriptions, manorial descents, lists of clergy, *etc.*

Two works deal with the history of personal names in Lincolnshire:

JENSEN, GILLIAN FELLOWES. *Scandinavian personal names in Lincolnshire and Yorkshire.* Copenhagen: I Kommission hos Akademisk forlag, 1968.

CAMERON, KENNETH. 'Bynames of location in Lincolnshire subsidy rolls', *Nottingham medieval studies* 32, 1988, 137-47.

There are many books and periodical articles dealing with particular aspects and periods of Lincolnshire history. The following list is very selective, and seeks to identify the more important general works, together with specialist works based on the types of sources genealogists use, and some items with a specific genealogical value. It is important that genealogists realise that the sources they rely on are also valuable for purposes of wider historical inquiry. The listing which follows is in rough chronological order.

HALLAM, H.E. *Settlement and society: a study of the early agrarian history of South Lincolnshire.* Cambridge: Cambridge University Press, 1965.

STENTON, FRANK MERRY. *Types of manorial structure in the northern Danelaw.* Oxford studies in social and legal history 7. Oxford: Clarendon Press, 1910. Study of Yorkshire, Derbyshire, Nottinghamshire, Leicestershire, Lincolnshire and Rutland, 10-12th c.

EVERSON, PAUL L., TAYLOR, C.C., & DUNN, C.J. *Change and continuity: rural settlement in North-West Lincolnshire.* H.M.S.O., 1991. Survey of medieval sites.

McLANE, BERNARD. 'A case study of violence and litigation in the early fourteenth century: the disputes of Robert Godsfield of Sutton-Le-Marsh', *Nottingham medieval studies* 28, 1984, 22-44.

STOREY, R.L. 'Lincolnshire and the Wars of the Roses', *Nottingham medieval studies* 14, 1970, 64-83.

HOLLAND, P. 'The Lincolnshire Rebellion of March 1470', *English historical review* 103, 1988, 849-69.

NICHOLS, JOHN GOUGH, ed. 'Chronicle of the rebellion in Lincolnshire, 1470', in *The Camden miscellany* vol.1. Camden Society old series 39, 1847.

THIRSK, JOAN. *English peasant farming: the agrarian history of Lincolnshire from Tudor to recent times.* Routledge & Kegan Paul, 1957.

MADDISON, A.R. 'Lincolnshire gentry during the sixteenth century', *A.A.S.R.P.* 22(2), 1894, 174-222. Includes genealogical notes on those involved in the Lincolnshire rising of 1536; also list of those supplying lances and horse in the muster of 1586.

THIRSK, JOAN. *Fenland farming in the sixteenth century.* Dept of English Local History occasional paper 3. Leicester: University College of Leicester, 1953.

BOWKER, MARGARET. 'Lincolnshire 1536: heresy, schism, or religious discontent?' in

BAKER, DAVID, ed. *Schism, heresy and religious protest.* Studies in church history 9. 1972, 195-212.

BUSH, L. 'Up for the Commonweal: the significance of tax grievances in the English rebellions of 1536', *English historical review* 106, 1991, 299-318.

DODDS, MADELEINE HOPE, & DODDS, RUTH. *The Pilgrimage of Grace, 1536-1537, and the Exeter conspiracy, 1538.* 2 vols. Frank Cass & Co., 1971. Originally published 1915.

GUNN, S.J. 'Peers, commons and gentry in the Lincolnshire revolt of 1536', *Past and present* 123, 1989, 52-79.

JAMES, M.E. 'Obedience and dissent in Henrician England: the Lincolnshire Rebellion, 1536', *Past and present* 48, 1970, 3-78. Reprinted in his *Society, politics and culture: studies in early modern England.* Cambridge: Cambridge University Press, 1986, 188-269.

WARD, ANNE. *The Lincolnshire Rising 1536.* Nottingham: Workers Educational Association, 1986.

BREARS, CHARLES. *Lincolnshire in the 17th and 18th centuries, compiled from national, county and parish records.* A. Brown & Sons, 1940.

MILLS, DENNIS R. 'The poor laws and the distribution of population c.1600-1860, with special reference to Lincolnshire', *Institute of British Geographers publications* 26, 1959, 185-95. Discussion of the effects of the law of settlement.

HOLDERNESS, B.A. 'Credit in English rural society before the nineteenth century, with special reference to the period 1650-1720', *Agricultural history review* 24, 1976, 97-109. Largely based on Lincolnshire probate inventories.

HOLDERNESS, B.A. 'Credit in a rural community, 1660-1800: Some neglected aspects of probate inventories', *Midland history* 3, 1975, 94-116.

GRIGG, DAVID. *The agricultural revolution in South Lincolnshire.* Cambridge: Cambridge University Press, 1966. 18-19th c.

PERKINS, J.A. *Sheep farming in eighteenth and nineteenth century Lincolnshire.* Occasional papers in Lincolnshire history and archaeology 4. Society for Lincolnshire History and Archaeology, 1977.

HOLDERNESS, B.A. 'The English land market in the eighteenth century: the case of Lincolnshire', *Economic history review* 2nd series **27**, 1974, 557-76. Study of changes in land ownership.

PERKINS, J.A. 'Harvest technology and labour supply in Lincolnshire and the East Riding of Yorkshire, 1750-1850', *Tools and tillage* 3(1), 1976, 47-58 & 64; 3(2), 1977, 125-35.

PERKINS, J.A. 'Tenure, tenant right, and agricultural progress in Lindsey, 1780-1850', *Agricultural history review* **23**, 1975, 1-22.

AMBLER, R.W. 'Baptism and Christening: custom and practice in nineteenth century Lincolnshire', *Local population studies* **12**, 1974, 25-7.

PERKINS, J.A. 'The Lincolnshire contraband tobacco trade after the Napoleonic wars', *Journal of transport history* N.S. **4**, 1977, 86-101.

HILL, SIR FRANCIS. 'Squire and parson in early Victorian Lincolnshire', *History* **58**, 1973, 337-49.

PERKINS, J.A. 'The prosperity of farming on the Lindsey uplands, 1813-37', *Agricultural history review* **24**, 1976, 126-43.

OBELKEVICH, JAMES. *Religion and rural society: South Lindsey, 1825-1875.* Oxford: Clarendon Press, 1976.

OLNEY, R.J. *Lincolnshire politics, 1832-1885.* Oxford University Press, 1973.

RAWDING, CHARLES. 'Society and place in nineteenth-century North Lincolnshire', *Rural history* **3**, 1992, 59-85.

RUSSELL, REX C. *The revolt of the field in Lincolnshire: the origins and early history of farm-workers trade unions.* Barton on Humber: National Union of Agricultural Workers, Lincolnshire County Committee, 1956. Primarily covers the 1870s.

STOVIN, JEAN, ed. *Journals of a Methodist farmer, 1871-1875.* Croom Helm, 1982. Diary of Cornelius Stovin; mentions many people.

Local Histories

Innumerable church, parish and local histories are available - far too many to list here. The following list primarily includes items having a particular genealogical value, which is specified, or have a wider general interest than is the norm with local histories. Much other local material is listed in more specific contexts below; consult the place index for these works.

Boston

THOMPSON, PISHEY. *The history and antiquities of Boston and the villages of Skirbeck, Fishtoft, Freiston, Butterwick, Benington, Leverton, Leake and Wrangle, comprising the Hundred of Skirbeck ...* Boston: John Noble, 1856. A parochial survey, giving much information on local families, manorial descents, extracts from original documents, *etc.* This is a greatly expanded version of:

THOMPSON, PISHEY. *Collections for a topographical and historical account of Boston and the Hundred of Skirbeck in the County of Lincoln.* Boston: the author, 1820.

Many more recent works are included in:

History of Boston series. 15 vols. Boston: Richard Kay Publications, 1970-77. Examples of publications in this series include:

DOVER, PERCY. *The early medieval history of Boston, A.D. 1086-1400.* History of Boston series **2**. 2nd ed. Boston: Richard Kay Publications for the History of Boston Project, 1972.

GARNER, A.A. *Boston and the Great Civil War, 1642-1651.* History of Boston series **7**. Boston: Richard Kay Publications, 1972. Includes the Boston protestation return, 1641/2, list of military burials, 1643-4, list of Edmund Syler's Company of foot, and biographical notes on prominent persons in Boston, 1642-51.

GARNER, A.A. *Boston: politics and the sea, 1652-1674.* History of Boston series **13**. Boston: Richard Kay Publications, 1975. Includes list of Boston ships and masters, 1660-73.

See also:

RIGBY, S.H. 'Sore decay and fair dwellings: Boston and urban decline in the later middle ages', *Midland history* **10**, 1985, 47-61.

RIGBY, STEPHEN. 'Urban society in early fourteenth-century England: the evidence of the lay subsidies', *Bulletin of the John Rylands University Library of Manchester* 72(3), 1990, 169-84. Based on the returns for Boston and Grimsby.

Conisholme

DUDDING, REGINALD C. 'Conisholme', *A.A.S.R.P.* 41(2), 1935, 119-40. Includes pedigrees of Copley, 16th c., Tempest, Berkeley and Pakenham, 16-17th c., and Dymock, 15-17th c., with list of early incumbents and patrons.

Corby

STEEL, DAVID I.A. *A Lincolnshire village: the parish of Corby Glen in its historical context.* Longman, 1979. Late 19-20th c., sociological study.

The Fens

BARLEY, M.W. *Lincolnshire and the Fens.* B.T. Batsford, 1952. Reprinted Wakefield: E.P. Publishing, 1972.

DARBY, H.C. *The changing Fenland.* Cambridge: C.U.P., 1983.

DARBY, HENRY C. *The draining of the Fens.* 2nd ed. Cambridge: C.U.P., 1956.

WHEELER, W.H. *History of the Fens of South Lincolnshire, being a description of the Rivers Witham and Welland and their tributaries, and an account of the reclamation, drainage and enclosure of the Fens adjacent thereto.* 2nd ed. Boston: J.M. Newcombe; London: Simpkin Marshall, 1896. Reprinted Stamford: Paul Watkins, 1990. Includes gazetteer.

STOVIN, G. 'A brief account of the drainage of the levells of Hatfield Chase and parts adjacent in the countys of York, Lincoln and Nottingham', *Yorkshire archaeological journal* 37, 1951, 385-91. Written in 1752; lists contemporary Huguenots, *etc.*

JACKSON, CHARLES. 'The Stovin manuscript', *Yorkshire archaeological and topographical journal* 7, 1882, 194-238. 17th c. transcripts of documents relating to the drainage of Hatfield Chase, in Yorkshire, Lincolnshire and Nottinghamshire; includes transcript of the Sandtoft Huguenot church register, 1643-85.

LINDLEY, KEITH. *Fenland riots and the English revolution.* Heinemann Educational, 1982.

HOLMES, C.' 'Drainers and Fenmen: the problem of popular political consciousness in the seventeenth century', in FLETCHER, ANTHONY, & STEVENSON, JOHN., eds. *Order and disorder in early modern England.* Cambridge University Press, 1985, 166-95.

KENNEDY, MARK E. 'Charles I and local government: the draining of the East and West Fens', *Albion* 15(1), 1983, 19-31.

KENNEDY, M.E. 'Fen drainage, the central government and local interest: Carleton and the gentlemen of South Holland', *Historical journal* 26, 1983, 15-37. Late 16th c.

Gainsborough

OOSTERVEEN, KARLA. 'Bastardy among the boatmen of Gainsborough, 1640-1812', *Local population studies* 25, 1980, 51-3. Demographic study, based on parish registers; includes notes on Awkland, Green, and Penney families.

Grantham

TURNOR, EDMUND. *Collections for the history of the town and soke of Grantham ...* William Miller, 1806. Includes various lists of benefactors, monumental inscriptions, parish register extracts, list of M.P.'s, various descents and pedigrees, *etc., etc.*

WHITE, MARTIN B. 'Family migration in Victorian Britain: the case of Grantham and Scunthorpe', *Local population studies* 41, 1988, 41-50. Based on the 1881 census.

Grimsby

GILLETT, EDWARD. *A history of Grimsby.* Oxford University Press, 1970.

RIGBY, S.H. 'Urban decline in the later middle ages: the reliability of the non-statistical evidence', *Urban history yearbook* 1984, 45-60. Study of Grimsby.

See also Boston

Horncastle

WALTER, J. CONWAY. *Records, historical and antiquarian, of parishes round Horncastle.* Horncastle: W.K. Morton, 1904. Parochial survey; many names.

Isle of Axholme

PECK, W. *A topographical account of the Isle of Axholme, being the West Division of the Wapentake of Manley in the County of Lincoln.* 2 vols. Doncaster: Thomas and Hunsley, 1815. Facsimile reprint Pisces Press, 1982.

Lincoln

HILL, SIR FRANCIS. *A short history of Lincoln.* Lincoln: Lincoln Civic Trust, 1979. Based on his other books.

HILL, SIR FRANCIS. *Medieval Lincoln.* Cambridge: Cambridge University Press, 1945. Reprinted Stamford: Watkins, 1990. Important; includes various 'citizens lists'.

HILL, J.W.F. *Tudor & Stuart Lincoln.* Cambridge: Cambridge University Press, 1956. Reprinted Stamford: Paul Watkins, 1991.

HILL, SIR FRANCIS. *Georgian Lincoln.* Cambridge: Cambridge University Press, 1966.

HILL, SIR FRANCIS. *Victorian Lincoln.* Cambridge: Cambridge University Press, 1974.

Potter Hanworth

NORGATE, KATE, & FOOTMAN, M.H. 'Some notes for a history of Potter Hanworth', *A.A.S.R.P.* 26(2), 1962, 369-93. Includes pedigree of D'Eyncourt, 11-14th c., list of rectors, a few deeds, *etc.*

Rippingale

HALL, ADRIAN. *Fenland worker peasants: the economy of smallholders at Rippingale, Lincolnshire, 1791-1871.* Agricultural history review supplement 1. Reading: British Agricultural History Society, 1992.

Scunthorpe

AMBLER, R.W., ed. *Workers and community: the people of Scunthorpe in the 1870s. A study based on the 1871 census returns.* Scunthorpe: Scunthorpe Museum Society, 1980.

Stamford

ELLIOTT, STUART. 'The open-field system of an urban community: Stamford in the nineteenth century', *Agricultural history review* 20, 1972, 155-69.

ROGERS, ALAN, ed. *The making of Stamford.* [Leicester]: Leicester University Press, 1965.

ROYAL COMMISSION ON HISTORICAL MONUMENTS. *An inventory of historical monuments: the town of Stamford.* H.M.S.O., 1977. Includes brief list of architects and craftsmen with biographical notes; also notes on monumental inscriptions.

2. BIBLIOGRAPHY AND ARCHIVES

A. General

There are a variety of libraries and record offices with holdings of interest to the Lincolnshire genealogist. Their various collections are described in:

THORNTON, RICHARD, ed. *Genealogical sources in Lincolnshire.* 2nd ed. Lincoln: L.F.H.S., 1993.

B. Bibliography

Lincolnshire lacks a comprehensive up to date listing of its historical literature. There are, however, two major bibliographical works. The catalogue of Lincoln's local history collection, published in 1904, remains important for identifying 19th century works on the county:

CORNS, A.R. *Bibliotheca Lincolniensis: a catalogue of the books, pamphlets, etc., relating to the City and County of Lincoln, preserved in the reference department of the City of Lincoln Public Library.* Lincoln: W.K. Morton, 1904.

For the City of Lincoln itself, a comprehensive bibliography has recently been published:

SHORT, D. MARY. *A bibliography of printed items relating to the City of Lincoln.* L.R.S. 79, 1990.

A number of briefer bibliographies are also available:

HOOPER, LINLEY. 'English county sources in the GSV library: Lincolnshire & Nottinghamshire', *Ancestor: quarterly journal of the Genealogical Society of Victoria* 22(1), 1994, 9-14.

Materials for a complete list of Lincolnshire topographical books. Supplement to *L.N.Q.* [189-.]

'Publications on the local history of the East Midlands', *Bulletin of local history: East Midlands region, passim.* Annual bibliography of historical publications on Leicestershire, Lincolnshire, Derbyshire, Nottinghamshire and Rutland. Title varies.

NANNESTAD, E., *et al.* 'Lincolnshire places: source material', *S.L.H.A. newsletter* 52-65, 1987-90, *passim.* Continued in *L.P.P.,* 1- , 1990- , *passim.* Bibliographical guide.

HOSTETTLER, EVE. 'Local history in Lincolnshire', *History workshop* **2**, 1976, 140-46. Brief review of Lincolnshire historical literature.
Village history: notes on some sources for the study of Lindsey villages. Local history handlist **2**. Gainsborough: Gainsborough Public Library, 1967.
The works of a leading Lincolnshire antiquarian are listed in:
BINNALL, P.B.G. 'A list of the principal writings of Edward Peacock, FSA', *L.H.* **2**(9), 1962, 1-6.
University theses are usually neglected by the genealogist. For a brief (now rather out of date) listing, see:
University and college theses in the local collection. Local history handbook **6**. 2nd ed. Gainsborough: Gainsborough Public Library, 1974.
The holdings of particular libraries have been described in a number of brief articles, *etc:*

Boston
HAY, KAREN. 'Family history holdings in Boston Library', *L.F.H.S.M.* **2**(2), 1991, 44-5.

Brigg
KETCHELL, CHRISTOPHER. *Brigg: sources of local information about Brigg.* Know your place bibliography **13**. Hull: Hull College of Further Education, Local History Unit, 1991.

Gainsborough
CREES, JANET. 'Records for family historians in Gainsborough Library', *L.F.H.S.M.* **4**(1), 1993, 6-7.
Gainsborough local studies: a handlist of books and pamphlets, illustrations and maps, relating to the town and its past, based on the Local and Brace collections of the Gainsborough Public Library. Gainsborough: the Library, 1965.
Lindsey towns and villages: books, pamphlets, and other material in the Gainsborough Public Library. Gainsborough: the Library, 1967. Catalogue.

Goole
KETCHELL, CHRISTOPHER. *A Goole bibliography: sources of local information about Goole.* Know your place local history bibliography **4**. Hull: Local History Archive Unit, 1989.

Grantham
BROWN, JOYCE. 'Sources for family historians in Grantham Library', *L.F.H.S.M.* **3**(2), 1992, 54-5.

Grimsby
WATTAM, DEREK. 'Family history resources at Grimsby Central Library', *L.F.H.S.M.* **2**(4), 1991, 132-3.

Humberside
HUMBERSIDE LIBRARIES. *A select bibliography of the County of Humberside.* Hull: Humberside Libraries and Amenities Dept., 1981.

Lincoln
NANNESTAD, ELEANOR. 'Family history in Lincoln Central Reference Library', *L.F.H.S.M.* **2**(1), 1991, 4-6.

Louth
JEFFERSON, J.K. *Richard William Goulding's collection: a handlist.* [Louth]: Lincolnshire Library Service, [1980]. Catalogue of an important collection of Lincolnshire books held at Louth.
NELLER, RUTH. 'Records for family historians in Louth Library', *L.F.H.S.M.* **3**(3), 1992, 96-7.

Scunthorpe
STOPPER, JANET. 'Family history research at Scunthorpe Central Library', *L.F.H.S.M.* **2**(3), 1991, 86-8.

Spalding
HAY, KAREN. 'Records for family historians in Spalding Library', *L.F.H.S.M.* **3**(1), 1992, 6-7.

Stamford
BROWN, JOYCE. 'Records for family historians in Stamford Library', *L.F.H.S.M.* **3**(4), 1992, 156-7.

C. *Archives*
For a general discussion of potentially useful historical source material in Lincolnshire, see:
THIRSK, JOAN. 'The content and sources of English agrarian history after 1500 with special reference to Lincolnshire', *L.H.* **2**(2), 1955, 31-44.

The major archives repository in Lincolnshire is the Lincolnshire Archives. Its genealogical collections are described in:
A guide to family history resources at Lincolnshire Archives. [Lincoln]: Lincolnshire County Council. Recreational Services, [199-].
For detailed lists of accessions, see:
LINCOLNSHIRE ARCHIVES COMMITTEE. *Archivists report.* Annual. The Committee, 1948-85. There are typescript reports available from 1937-47 and 1986 onwards. Printed reports are indexed in:
LINCOLNSHIRE ARCHIVES COMMITTEE. *Index: archivists reports, 1948-1958.* [Lincoln]: the Committee, 1961. A further index *1958-1968* was published in 1975.
See also:
'Accessions to archives', *Midland history* **1-3**, 1971-6, *passim.*
There are a number of general, but dated, descriptions of the archives:
FINCH, MARY. 'Five years of the Lincolnshire Archives Office', *L.H.* **2**(11), 1964, 29-37.
VARLEY, JOAN. 'Local archives of Great Britain, VI: the Lincolnshire Archives Committee', *Archives* **1**(6), 1951, 5-16.
VARLEY, JOAN. 'The Lincolnshire Archives Office', *Bulletin of local history: East Midlands region* **5**, 1970, 1-13.
'Other collections deposited with the Lincoln Diocesan Record Offices and the Lincolnshire Archives Committee, 1947-9', *L.A.A.S.R.P.* N.S. **4**, 1951, 80.
'The Lindsey muniment room', *Lincolnshire magazine* **2**(1), 1934, 5-6. Brief note.
For the Lincoln diocesan archives, see below, section 13.
There are a number of other important archive repositories in Lincolnshire. See:

South Humberside
WILSON, JOHN. *Guide to the South Humberside Area Archive Office.* [Grimsby]: Humberside County Council, 1993.
WILSON, JOHN. 'Oral history recordings in the South Humberside Area Archive Office', *L.P.P.* **13**, 1993, 15-16. List.

Spalding
SPALDING GENTLEMEN'S SOCIETY. *Annual report* 1930- . Includes lists of new accessions. There may be earlier issues, but this is the earliest seen.

D. *Family History Societies*
There are two family history societies covering Lincolnshire. The predecessor of the Lincolnshire Family History Society was discussed in a now very dated article:
RATCLIFFE, RICHARD. 'Society for Lincolnshire History and Archaeology Family History Committee', *Family tree magazine* **3**(1), 1986, 17.
For the Isle of Axholme, see:
'The Isle of Axholme Family History Society', *Family tree magazine* **6**(12), 1990, 21.

13

3. PERIODICALS AND NEWSPAPERS

A variety of periodicals of relevance to the Lincolnshire genealogist are available. The newsletters and journals of the various family history societies are of particular importance; in addition to the brief but useful articles they carry, they also provide news of genealogical events and projects – and, most importantly, they enable subscribers to make contact with others researching the same names. The earliest such newsletter was:

The Society for Lincolnshire History and Archaeology. Family History Section newsletter. 12 issues. 1978-81. Continued by:
Lincolnshire family historian. 7 vols. Lincoln: S.L.H.A., 1981-1990. Includes members interests, notes on archives.

In 1990, the family history section of the S.L.H.A. was dissolved, and a new society formed. Its journal is:
Lincolnshire Family History Society [magazine]. 1990-
For the Isle of Axholme, see:
The Islonian: the journal of the Isle of Axholme Family History Society. 1987-

There are a number of historical journals of importance to the Lincolnshire genealogist. Their publishing history has, however, been rather kaleidoscopic, with various changes to both the titles of journals and the names of publishers. The most important journal currently being published is *Lincolnshire history and archaeology.* Its various incarnations are as follows:
The Lincolnshire magazine. 4 vols. Lincoln: Lindsey Local History Society, 1932-9. Continued by:
The Lincolnshire historian. 2 vols. Lincoln: Lincolnshire Local History Society, 1947-65. Continued by:
Lincolnshire history and archaeology. Lincolnshire Local History Society, (Society for Lincolnshire History and Archaeology from 1975), 1966-
Newsletters, some of which contain information of permanent value, have also emanated from the same publishers:
The local historian. 46 issues. Lincoln: Lindsey Local History Society, 1935-45. Brief articles and notes.

SOCIETY FOR LINCOLNSHIRE HISTORY AND ARCHAEOLOGY. *Newsletter.* 65 issues. 1974-90. Continued by:
Lincolnshire past and present. [Lincoln]: S.L.H.A., 1990-
Vital material for the genealogist has been published by the Lincolnshire Architectural and Archaeological Society, in conjunction with a number of other county societies. See:
Reports and papers of the Associated Architectural Societies. 40 vols. 1850-1930. Continued by:
Reports and papers of the architectural and archaeological societies of the counties of Lincoln and Northampton. 2 vols. 1934-7. Continued by:
Lincolnshire Architectural and Archaeological Society reports & papers. New series. 1939-64.
Numerous editions of original sources – many of them individually listed below – are available in an important record series:
The publications of the Lincoln Record Society. 1911-
For an important regional journal which includes listings of new local publications as well as useful articles, see:
Bulletin of local history: East Midlands region. 25 issues. University of Nottingham: East Midlands Region, 1966-90. Title varies. Includes brief notes on accessions to local record offices, extensive book reviews, notes on research work in progress, *etc.* Covers Derbyshire, Leicestershire, Lincolnshire, Nottinghamshire and Rutland, and Northamptonshire from vol.12. This is indexed in:
'Index of volumes I-VIII', *Bulletin of local history: East Midland region* **8**, 1973, 139-51.
Bulletin of local history: East Midland Region. Index to volumes IX-XIII. [Nottingham]: University of Nottingham, [1979?]
The *Bulletin* is continued by:
East Midland historian. Nottingham: University of Nottingham, 1992-
Two important journals of *notes and queries* covering Lincolnshire contained much information of family history, including numerous extracts from original sources; many of these 'notes' are listed in the appropriate place below:

Lincolnshire notes and queries: a quarterly journal ... 24 vols. Horncastle: W.K. Morton, 1889-1936.

Fenland notes and queries: a quarterly antiquarian journal for the counties of Huntingdon, Cambridge, Lincoln, Northampton, Norfolk and Suffolk. 7 vols. Peterborough: [ ], 1889-1909.

For Stamford history, reference may be made to:

The Stamford historian. 6 vols. Nottingham: University of Nottingham for the Stamford Survey Group, 1977-82. This is indexed in:

The Stamford historian: name and subject index, volumes 1-4. Nottingham: University of Nottingham, [1980?]

Newspapers carry much information of interest to genealogists – especially in their births, marriages and deaths columns. Those which have been published in Lincolnshire are listed, with locations, in:

GORDON, RUTH. *Newsplan: report of the Newsplan project in the East Midlands, April 1987-July 1988.* British Library, 1989. This also covers Cambridgeshire, Derbyshire, Leicestershire, Norfolk, Northamptonshire, Nottinghamshire and Suffolk. See also:

TOLLEY, B.H. 'Newspapers of the East Midlands up to 1920', *Bulletin of local history: East Midlands Region* 4, 1969, 62-73. Summary list; no locations. Covers Derbyshire, Leicestershire, Lincolnshire, Nottinghamshire and Rutland.

For Boston newspapers, see:

ROBINSON, LIONEL. *Boston's newspapers.* History of Boston series 11. Boston: Richard Kay Publications, 1974. Includes a detailed list.

4. PEDIGREE COLLECTIONS AND HERALDRY

Much work on Lincolnshire genealogy has already been completed. An extensive collection of pedigrees, based on the work of A.S. Larken, is printed in:

MADDISON, A.R., ed. *Lincolnshire pedigrees.* 4 vols. Publications of the Harleian Society, visitations, **50-52 & 55.** 1902-6.

See also:

F., W.E. 'Some Lincolnshire pedigrees from the plea rolls', *L.N.Q.* **4,** 1896, 37-45. Medieval collection.

'An index to the book of pedigrees compiled by the late Mr W.S. Hesledon', *L.N.Q.* **3,** 1893, 101-3.

REDSHAW, E.J. 'Index to Everard Green's manuscript pedigrees of Lincolnshire families', *Family history* 5(28/29); N.S. **4/5,** 1968, 109-16; **6/7,** 1968, 191-207. Lists collection of pedigrees held by Spalding Gentlemen's Society.

Birth briefs. Sleaford: S.L.H.A., F.H.C., 1982-4. 2 vols. Brief pedigrees.

In the sixteenth and seventeenth centuries, the Heralds undertook 'visitations' of the counties in order to determine the rights of the gentry to bear coat armour. In so doing, they compiled pedigrees of most of the leading families in Lincolnshire. Their compilations form the oldest collections of pedigrees for the country, and various extracts from them and studies based on them have been published. See:

METCALFE, WALTER C. *The visitation of the County of Lincoln in 1562-4.* George Bell & Sons, 1881.

'The visitation of Lincolnshire, 1562-4, made by Robert Cooke *alias* Chester, deputy and marshall to W. Henry, Clarenceux', *Genealogist* **3,** 1879, 337-76; **4,** 1880, 18-33, 110-17, 179-93 & 245-77; **5,** 1881, 33-60 & 114.

METCALFE, WALTER C., ed. *The visitation of the County of Lincoln, 1592.* George Bell & Son, 1882.

'The visitation of Lincolnshire, 1592, made by Richard Lee, Richmond Herald, for Robert Cooke, Clarenceaux', *Genealogist* **5,** 1881, 187-92 & 308-17; **6,** 1882, 140-61 & 256-93.

GIBBONS, A. *Notes on the visitation of Lincolnshire, 1634.* Lincoln: James Williamson, 1898. Includes many extracts from parish registers, with monumental inscriptions, *etc.,* also indexes of *Wills and administrations in the Court of the Dean and Chapter of Lincoln, 1534-1780,* and of *Wills in the Consistory Court of Lincoln,* covering 1506-31.

GREEN, EVERARD, ed. *The visitation of of the County of Lincoln made by Sir Edward Bysshe, knight, Clarenceux King of arms, in the year of our lord 1666.* L.R.S. **3,** 1917.

PEACOCK, EDWARD. 'An index to the Lincolnshire names contained in the Visitation of Yorkshire, 1665-6', *L.N.Q.* **3,** 1893, 86-9.

For lists of the county gentry and aristocracy, see:

WELBY, ALFRED J. 'Lincolnshire in the Barons' War, 1264-1266', *L.N.Q.* **15,** 1919, 52-9. Lists rebel barons.

MADDISON, A.R. 'Inheritors in Co.Lincoln, 1550-1650', *L.N.Q.* **10,** 1909, 56-62. Lists the county gentry.

WELBY, ALFRED C.E. 'Baronets of Lincolnshire, 1720', *L.N.Q.* **14,** 1916-17, 213-5. List from Cox's *Magna Britannia.*

Heraldry

Brownlow

CUST, LADY ELIZABETH. 'Armorial bookplate: Sir William Brownlow, 1698', *M.G.H.* 2nd series **1,** 1886, 221.

Dalison

'Dalison: funeral certificates', *M.G.H.* 2nd series **2,** 1888, 117-8. Also of Kent; 17th c.

'Grant of crest to William Dalison, gent., 3 and 4 Philip and Mary', *M.G.H.* 2nd series **2,** 1888, 105.

Johnson

'Grants and confirmations of arms and crests', *M.G.H.* 5th series **9,** 1935-7, 126-8. Includes Johnson of Gainsborough, 1579.

More

'Exemplification of arms to John and Edmond More, by Robert Cooke, Clarenceaux, 1593', *M.G.H.* **1,** 1868, 309-10.

Peake

'Grants and confirmations of arms and crests', *M.G.H.* 5th series **9,** 1935-7, 42-3. Peake, 1562.

Tupholme

'Exemplification of arms and grant of crest to William Tupholme of Boston, Co.Lincoln, 1562', *M.G.H.* 4th series **1,** 1906, 41-2.

Walpole

'Grant of augmentation to Sir John Walpole of Dunston, Co.Lincoln, knight, by Sir Edward Walker, Garter, 1646', *Genealogist* **1,** 1877, 1.

Welby

'Grant of crest, by William Hervy, Clarenceaux, to Richard Welby of Halstead, in the county of Lincoln, 1562', *M.G.H.* **1,** 1868, 249-50.

5. GENEALOGICAL DIRECTORIES AND BIOGRAPHICAL DICTIONARIES

A. Genealogical directories
Amongst the most valuable sources of genealogical information are the directories of members interests published by the various family history societies. For Lincolnshire, see:
PERKINS, JOHN P. *Lincolnshire families directory 2.* 1 fiche. [Lincoln]: [L.F.H.S.], 1992.
PERKINS, JOHN P. *Lincolnshire families directory.* Doncaster: F.F.H.S. for the Isle of Axholme F.H.S., 1990.
Directory of members interests, 1984-1985. S.L.H.A., F.H.C., 1986.

B. Biographical dictionaries
Brief biographies/obituaries of Lincolnshire men are contained in a number of local biographical dictionaries. These are listed here by date of publication.
SIMPSON, JUSTIN. *Obituary and records for the counties of Lincoln, Rutland & Northampton, from the commencement of the present century to the end of 1859.* Stamford: William R. Newcomb, 1861. Brief obituaries of numerous 'worthies'.
WATKINS, MORGAN G. *The worthies of Lincolnshire.* Elliot Stock, 1885. List of 'worthies', with brief biographical notes.
PRESS, C.A. MANNING. *Lincolnshire leaders, social and political.* Jarrold & Sons, 1894.
Lincolnshire at the opening of the twentieth century. Pikes new century series **22.** Brighton: W.T. Pike & Co., 1907. Includes W.T. Pike ed. *Contemporary biographies* which has been reprinted as:
HUNT, A., & PIKE, W.T. *A dictionary of Edwardian biography: Lincolnshire.* Edinburgh: Peter Bell, 1987.
GASKELL, ERNEST. *Lincolnshire leaders, social and political.* Queenhithe, 1908.
Who's who in Lincolnshire. Worcester: Ebenezer Baylis & Son, 1935.
KETTERINGHAM, JOHN. *Lincolnshire people.* Kings England Press, forthcoming.

6. OCCUPATIONAL INFORMATION

There are many works offering biographical information on people of particular occupations or status. These are listed here. For clergymen, see below, section 13, for teachers, section 17, for members of parliament, sheriffs, and other governmental officers, section 14. This list complements the list provided in my *Occupational sources for genealogists.*

Actors
Records of plays and players in Lincolnshire, 1300-1585. Malone Society collections **8,** 1969 (1974).

Airmen
INGHAM, M.J. *The Air Force memorials of Lincolnshire.* [3rd ed.] Nettleham: Beckside Design, 1987. Originally published as *A guide to ...*

Antiquarians
MOORE, WILLIAM. *The Gentlemen's Society at Spalding: its origin and progress.* William Pickering, 1851. Includes extensive list of members, 18-19th c.
OWEN, DOROTHY M., ed. *The minute book of the Spalding Gentlemen's Society, 1712-1755.* L.R.S. **73,** 1981. Includes names of members, etc.

Apothecaries
BURNBY, J.G.L. 'Local studies of the English apothecary', *L.H.A.* **24,** 1989, 17-27. Includes notes on the issuers of Lincolnshire apothecaries' tokens, and a pedigree of Clarke of Grantham and Loughborough, Leicestershire, 17-18th c.

Apprentices
WESTLAND, RICHARD A. *Apprentices and masters of Boston, Lincolnshire, 1545-1717 as recorded in the Assembly minutes of the Corporation of Boston.* Fiche. [ ]: L.F.H.S., 1991.
COLE, ANNE, & MACKINDER, A. *Lincoln city apprentices register, volume 1 (L1/5/2).* 1 fiche. Lincoln: L.F.H.S., 1990. Covers 1640-1765.

COLE, ANNE, & MACKINDER, ALICE. *Index to the Lincoln city apprentices registers.* 2 fiche. Lincoln: L.F.H.S., 1992. Covers 1765-1867.

COLE, ANNE. 'Lincoln City apprentices index vol.2', *L.F.H.S.M.* 3(3), 1992, 119. Brief note on the previous work.
See also Carpenters, Fishermen, and Metal Tradesmen

Bankers
DAVIS, S.N. *Banking in Boston.* History of Boston series 14. Boston: Richard Kay Publications, 1976. General account.

PORTER, H. 'Lincolnshire private bankers', *Lincolnshire magazine* 3, 1936-8, 138-42 & 165-70. 19th c.

PORTER, H. 'Old private bankers of North Lincolnshire', *Lincolnshire magazine* 2, 1934-6, 289-96.

Bankrupts
HANSON, P.H. 'Lincolnshire bankrupts', *L.F.H.S.M.* 2(2), 1991, 53; 2(3), 1991, 103; 2(4), 1991, 131; 3(1), 1992, 16; 3(2), 1992, 75; 3(3), 1992, 123; 3(4), 1992, 150; 4(1), 1993, 22. List, 1818-58.

Booksellers
See Printers and Booksellers

Building Tradesmen
SIMPSON, W. DOUGLAS, ed. *The building accounts of Tattershall Castle, 1434-1472.* L.R.S. 55. 1960. Gives many names of building tradesmen, creditors, *etc.*

Carpenters
MARSH, BOWER. 'Apprentices from the County of Lincoln bound at Carpenters Hall, London, 1654-1694', *L.N.Q.* 13, 1914, 66-9. List.

Clockmakers
TEBBUTT, LAURENCE. *Stamford clocks & watches & their makers.* Stamford: Dolby Brothers, 1975. Includes list of makers.

Cricketers
BARTLETT, *et al. Lincolnshire cricketers, 1828-1993.* Nottingham: Association of Cricket Statisticians, forthcoming.

DODS, H. 'Personalities in Lincolnshire County cricket', *Lincolnshire magazine* 3, 1936-8, 251-4.

Customs Officers
RIGBY, S.H. 'The customs administration at Boston in the reign of Richard II', *Bulletin of the Institute of Historical Research* 58, 1985, 12-24. Includes lists of collectors, 1377-99.

Deserters
'Deserters and absconders', *L.F.H.S.M.* 3(2), 1992, 68-9. Extracts from the *Lincoln, Rutland & Stamford Mercury,* late 18th-early 19th c., mainly relating to persons deserting employers or families.

Fishermen
BOSWELL, DAVID, *Sea fishing apprentices of Grimsby.* Grimsby: Grimsby Public Libraries and Museum, 1974. General study; includes a list of apprentices who died whilst serving their indentures, 1880-1923.

WILSON, JOHN, ed. *Sea going apprentices of Grimsby: index 1879 to 1937.* Grimsby: South Humberside Area Archive Office, 1992. Index of a register of apprentices.

WILSON, JOHN. *Sea going apprentices of Grimsby. Part 1. Index of registers of sea fishing apprentices, 1880-1937. Part 2. Index of sea fishing and merchant apprentices, 1879-1919 from other sources.* Grimsby: Humberside County Council, 1990.

'Was your ancestor a sea fishing apprentice?' *L.F.H.S.M.* 1(3), 1990, 57. Note on index to Grimsby apprenticeship registers, 1880-1937.

Footballers
TRIGGS, LES, *et al. Grimsby Town: a complete record, 1878-1989.* Derby: Breedon Books Sport, 1989. Lists players.

LAMMING, DOUGLAS. *A who's who of Grimsby Town AFC, 1890-1985.* Beverley: Hutton Press, 1985.

NANNESTAD, D., & NANNESTAD, I. *Who's who of Lincoln City Football Club.* Yore Publications, forthcoming. Title to be confirmed.

Freeholders

TUNNARD, MICHAEL, ed. 'Kirton Wapentake: freeholders "who hath to the vallue of 10 pounds p. annum or upward", 14 Nov. 1715', *L.H.* **1**, 1947-53, 238-40. List.

Freemasons

BATES, ANDERSON. *The history of Freemasonry in Grimsby from its introduction to 1892.* Grimsby: Albert Gait, 1892. Includes various lists of freemasons.

DIXON, WILLIAM. *A history of freemasonry in Lincolnshire: being a record of all extinct and existing lodges, chapters, &c., ... together with biographical notices of the Provincial Grand Masters and other eminent masons of the County.* Lincoln: James Williamson, 1894.

LINNELL, R.J. *A history of Stamford freemasonry: a study of the Lodge of Merit no 466, and of early freemasonry in Stamford.* Stamford: Stamford Masonic Centre, 1982, Includes list of masters, 1840-1982, *etc.*

Gallows Owners

'Private gallows in Lincolnshire c.1274', *L.N.Q.* **23**, 1936, 108-13. Lists owners of gallows.

Gaolers

'Lincolnshire prisons', *L.N.Q.* **22**, 1934, 84-90. List of prisons, naming gaolers, 1801-12.

Huntsmen

COLLINS, G.E. *History of the Brocklesby hounds, 1700-1901.* Sampson Low, Marston & Company, 1902. Includes many notes on huntsmen, with a pedigree of Pelham and Anderson, 17-19th c.

Knights

'Knights of Lincolnshire summoned to come to the King at Berwick on Tweed, with horses and armour. Order dated 12 March 1300-1', *L.N.Q.* **20**, 1929, 125-8. List. Also includes list of c.1308-14.

G[IBBONS], G.S. 'Lincolnshire knights', *L.N.Q.* **20**, 1929, 104-8. List of knights fit for military service, 1324.

'Crusaders in Lincolnshire', *F.N.Q.* **6**, 1904-6, 97-100. List, c.1197.

Labourers

JOHNSTON, J.A. 'The family and kin of the Lincolnshire labourer in the eighteenth century', *L.H.A.* **14**, 1979, 47-52. Based on probate records.

Launderers

ELVIN, LAURENCE. *Jacksons of Lincoln: dyers, cleaners, launderers, 1791-1991.* 2nd ed. Lincoln: Jacksons Lincoln Laundry, 1991. Includes list of long-serving staff members.

Medical Men

MILLS, DENNIS R. 'A *directory* of Lincolnshire medical men in the late eighteenth century: two original sources', *L.H.A.* **23**, 1988, 59-62. List based on the *Medical register,* 1779, 1780 and 1783, and the *Universal British directory,* 1790s.

Merchants

See Ships Masters

Metal Tradesmen

'Lincolnshire apprentices to the metal trades in Hallamshire', *L.F.H.S.M.* **4**(1), 1993, 31-3. List, 17-19th c.

Millers

WAILES, REX. 'Lincolnshire windmills', *Newcomen Society ... transactions* **28**, 1951-3, 245-53; **29**, 1953-5, 103-22. Includes some names of millers.

Nurserymen

EAGLE, EDGAR C. 'Some light on the beginning of the Lincolnshire bulb industry', *L.H.* **1**(5), 1950, 220-29. Includes some names of nurserymen, 1892, *etc.*

Organ Builders and Organists

ELVIN, LAURENCE. *Bishop and Son, organ builders: the story of J.C. Bishop and his successors.* Lincoln: the author, 1984. Includes chapters on the Bishop and Suggate families, and on 'master organ builders trained at Bishop and Son', *etc.*

ELVIN, LAURENCE. *Family enterprise: the story of some North country organ builders.* Lincoln: the author, 1986. Much of the book is Lincolnshire based, it includes a chapter on 'the organists of Lincoln Cathedral, 1794-1986', with much biographical information.

Patients

RATCLIFFE, RICHARD. 'Lincoln County Hospital in-patients register, 1798-1808', *S.L.H.A.F.H.S.N.* 5(7), 1987, 23-4. Includes extracts.

Pharmacists

ELLIS, R. 'Pharmacy in Stamford a century ago', *Pharmaceutical historian: newsletter of the British Society for the History of Pharmacy* 1, 1967, 4-8.

Pipe Makers

COMRIE, A.C. 'The clay tobacco pipe industry in Stamford', in DAVEY, PETER, ed. *The archaeology of the clay tobacco pipe, 1: Britain: the Midlands and Eastern England.* BAR British series 63, 1979, 187-228. Includes detailed notes on pipemakers.

WALKER, IAIN C., & WELLS, PETER K. 'Regional varieties of clay tobacco pipe-markings in Eastern England', in DAVEY, PETER, ed. *The archeology of the clay tobacco pipe, 1: Britain: the Midlands and Eastern England.* BAR British series 63, 1979, 3-66. Appendices name pipemakers in Nottingham and Lincolnshire, *etc.*

WELLS, P.K. 'The pipe-makers of Lincolnshire', in DAVEY, PETER, ed. *The archaeology of the clay tobacco pipe, 1: Britain, the Midlands and Eastern England.* BAR British series 63, 1979, 123-69. Includes biographical notes on many pipemakers, with probate inventories of John Fox of Spalding, 1671, James Harford of Boston, 1676, Isaac Bilby of Spalding, 1728 and Matthew Heblethwaite of Lincoln, 1729.

WELLS, PETER. 'The clay pipe makers of Boston', in *Aspects of nineteenth century Boston and District.* History of Boston series 8. Boston: Richard Kay Publications, 1972, 13-17. Brief discussion, with some names.

WELLS, P.K. 'The excavation of a 19th-century clay tobacco pipe kiln in Boston, Lincolnshire', *L.H.A.* 5, 1970, 21-7. Includes list of Boston pipemakers.

Printers and Booksellers

GOULDING, R.D. W. *Notes on Louth printers and booksellers of the eighteenth century.* Louth: Goulding & Son, 1917.

Rowers

PUCKERING, ROBERT COMINS, & DAWBER, EDMUND. *A short history of the Gainsborough Rowing Club, from its foundation in 1863 to its diamond jubilee in 1923.* Gloucester: John Bellows, 1923. Includes various lists of members, *etc.*

Seamen

See Fishermen

Servants

'Receipts for the men and women's wages due at Lady Day 1740, paid at Brox[n] Aug 30, 1740', *L.N.Q.* 16, 1921, 203-7.

Shareholders

GILLETT, E. 'Grimsby and the Haven Company', *L.H.* 1, 1947-53, 359-74. Includes list of shareholders, 1805.

Shipowners

JONES, STEPHANIE. 'Shipowning in Boston, Lincolnshire, 1836-1848', *Mariners' mirror* 65, 1979, 339-49. General discussion; few names.

Ships Masters

HINTON, R.W.K., ed. *The port books of Boston, 1601-1640.* L.R.S. 50, 1956. Gives many names of ships' masters and merchants, *etc.*

Shopkeepers

BARLEY, L.B., & BARLEY, M.W. 'Lincolnshire shopkeepers in the sixteenth and seventeenth centuries', *L.H.* 2(9), 1962, 7-21. Based on probate inventories.

Slate Engravers

NEAVE, DAVID, & HERON, VANESSA. 'Kesteven slate headstones and their engravers, 1700-1825', *L.H.A.* 4, 1969, 3-18. Biographical dictionary.

Smack Builders

HALLETT, GLADYS C. 'The smackbuilders of Grimsby', *L.P.P.* 6, 1991/2, 9. Includes list, 1871-83.

Soldiers and Militiamen

Many men of Lincolnshire served in the army, or in the militia, and much information on them is available in the various regimental histories, *etc.*, which have been compiled.

These cannot all be listed here. The works listed below include only those publications which list officers and men, or provide other information of genealogical value. It is arranged in rough chronological order.

'Militia assessments at Deeping St.James', *F.N.Q.* **5**, 1901-3, 22-28 & 60-64. Names of those liable to serve, 1683, 1715 and 1716.

'Lincolnshire Militia', *Notes and queries* **165**, 1934, 355-6. See also 318. Lists officers, 1759.

WELBY, ALFRED. 'Officers of the N. and S. Lincs Militia, 1779', *L.N.Q.* **24**, 1936, 24-6. List.

WELBY, ALFRED. 'Officers of Lincolnshire Corps, 1795', *L.N.Q.* **20**, 1929, 52-4. List.

D., M.M. 'Norman Cross Barracks', *F.N.Q.* **2**, 1892-4, 200-202. See also 216-8, 271 & 405. Names officers of the Royal South Lincoln Regiment of Militia, 1797.

'Isle militia lists', *Islonian* **2**(6), 1990, 24; **3**(4), 1991, 23; **4**(2), 1992, 11; **4**(3), 1992, 25. Lists for West Butterwick, Belton, Haxey and Epworth.

FANE, W.K. 'The orderly book of Captain Daniel Hebb's company in the Loveden Volunteers (Lincolnshire), 1803-8', *Journal of the Society of Army Historical Research* **4**, 1925, 149-61. Includes list of officers.

WILLIAMS, J. ROBERT. 'Lincolnshire veterans of the 5th Foot', *S.L.H.A.F.H.S.N.* **2**(4), 1983, 7-13. List, early 19th c.

LEE, ALBERT. *The history of the Tenth Foot (the Lincolnshire Regiment).* 2 vols. Aldershot: Gale & Polden, 1911. Includes an alphabetical list of officers, 1865-1910, comp. A.C. Chamier.

Soldiers died in the Great War, 1914-1918; part 15: the Lincolnshire Regiment. H.M.S.O., 1921. Reprinted Polstead: J.B. Hayward & Son, 1989.

BRYANT, PETER. *Grimsby chums: the story of the 10th Lincolnshires in the Great War.* Humberside Heritage Publications 21. Hull: Humberside Leisure Services, 1990. Includes roll of honour.

PACEY, RON. 'Manchester Regiment 1914-1918 war casualties', *L.F.H.S.M.* **3**(2), 1992, 60-62. Lists men born in Lincolnshire.

SIMPSON, C.R. *The history of the Lincolnshire Regiment, 1914-1918 ...* Medici Society, 1931. Includes extensive roll of honour, *etc.*

GATES, L.C. *The history of the 10th Foot, 1919-50.* ed. J.A.A. Griffin. Aldershot: Gale and Polden, 1953. Royal Lincolnshire Regiment; includes roll of honour, *etc.*

Stone Masons

RUSSELL, REX C. *Headstones in Lincolnshire as works of art and as evidence of craftsmanship.* 2 vols. Barton on Humber: Workers Educational Association, 1981-2. No inscriptions, but includes lists of stone masons, 1855-82.

Swan Owners

TICEHURST, N.F. 'The swan marks of Lincolnshire', *A.A.S.R.P.* **42**(1), 1936, 59-141. List of swan owners, 15-17th c.

TICEHURST, N.F. 'Swan marks', *Lincolnshire magazine* **3**, 1936-8, 115-22. Includes list of 70 swan owners, 16th c.

'Swan marks in Lincolnshire', *F.N.Q.* **5**, 1901-3, 277-9. Lists swan owners, early 16th c.

Tobacco Manufacturers

WRIGHT, NEIL R. 'Tobacco manufacturing in Lincolnshire', *Industrial archaeology* **7**(1), 1970, 1-33.

Tradesmen

HOLDERNESS, B.A. 'Rural tradesmen, 1660-1850: a regional study in Lindsey', *L.H.A.* **7**, 1972, 77-83. Based on probate inventories. In an age when coins were in short supply, many tradesmen issued their own tokens. Studies of these yield much information of genealogical value; see:

SHEPPARD, THOMAS. *A list of the seventeenth century tokens of Lincolnshire in the Hull Museum, with descriptions of hitherto unpublished tokens and varieties.* Hull Museum publications **79**, 1911. Reprinted from *Transactions of the Hull Scientific and Field Naturalists' Club* **4**(3), 1911, 115-44. Also published in *Transactions of the Yorkshire Numismatic Society* **1**, 1909-15, supplement, 115-44. See also **2**, 1916-25, 47-9.

SIMPSON, JUSTIN. *A list of the Lincolnshire series of tradesmens tokens & town pieces of the seventeenth century, with biographical and genealogical notes.* Bemrose and Sons, 1872.

SMITH, ARTHUR. 'The seventeenth century tokens of Lincolnshire', *L.N.Q.* **14**, 1916-17, 130-33, 161-6 & 193-6; **15**, 1918-19, 65-70 & 161-9; **20**, 1929, 17-20 & 82-6; **21**, 1931, 17-21, 40-47 & 51-7.

SMITH, ARTHUR. 'Lincolnshire town and trade tokens issued in the 17th century', *Lincolnshire magazine* **1**(9), 1934, 284-8.

TOWNSEND, T.W. *Seventeenth century tradesmen's tokens of Lincolnshire: the issuers.* Occasional papers 2. Lincoln: Lincolnshire Museum, 1983.

KETTERINGHAM, STEPHEN. 'Lincolnshire tokens', *L.P.P.* **2**, 1990/91, 9-10.

GOULDING, RD. WM. *Louth tradesmen's tokens: a paper read before the Louth Naturalists Antiquarian and Literary Society.* Louth: Goulding & Son, 1914.

7. FAMILY HISTORIES AND PEDIGREES

A considerable amount of research on particular Lincolnshire families has been published, and is listed here. This includes complete histories, brief notes, pedigrees, *etc.* Biographies, in general, are not included; nor are works which have not been published. Many of the items listed also contain information on related families; consequently, even if your surname is not directly mentioned here, there may be information of relevance in some of these works.

Adye
See Cholmeley

Allen
HIGGINS, C.A. 'Pedigree of Allen of Lincolnshire', *M.G.H.* 5th series **8**, 1932-4, 211-14. 16-17th c.

Ambler
GREEN, EVERARD. 'Pedigree of Ambler of Kirton in Holland, and of Holyrood in the parish of Spalding, both in Co.Lincoln', *M.G.H.* 4th series **1**, 1906, 126-8. 17th c.

Amcotts
MADDISON, A.R. 'Amcotts family', *L.N.Q.* **8**, 1905, 61-3. Includes pedigree, 16-17th c.

Amundeville
CLAY, C.T. 'The family of Amundeville', *L.A.A.S.R.P.* N.S. **3**, 1945, 109-37. Medieval; includes folded pedigree.

WASHINGTON, S.H. LEE. 'The Washingtons and the Amundevilles', *New England historical and genealogical register* **100**, 1946, 305-8. Medieval Amundeville family.

Amyot
AMYOT, T.E. 'Pedigree of the Huguenot family of Amyot', *M.G.H.* 3rd series **2**, 1898, 26-30. 16-19th c., also of Norfolk and France.

Arnold
T., E.B. 'The Arnolds of Coleby', *L.N.Q.* **4**, 1896, 91-4. 16th c.

Ashby

FOSTER, C.W. 'Ashby de la Launde and Temple Bruer, and the families of Ashby and De La Launde', *L.N.Q.* **17,** 1923, 131-49. Includes pedigree, medieval.

Ashton

ASHTON, M.J. 'The Ashton family of Lincolnshire, chairmakers', *S.L.H.A. newsletter* **54,** 1987, 22-5. 19th c.

GREEN, EVERARD. 'Pedigree of the family of Ashton of Spalding and Grantham, Co.Lincoln', *Genealogist* **2,** 1878, 327-31. 15-18th c.

Atkinson

ATKINSON, HAROLD WARING. *The families of Atkinson of Roxby (Lincs) and Thorne, and Dearman of Braithwaite, and families connected with them, especially Atkinson-Busfeild, Barnes, Beavington, Birchall, Edwards, Miller, Neave, Ransome, Rooke, Sessions, Sinclair, Somerford, Stanley, Waring, Wykeham.* Northwood, Middlesex: the author, 1933. Includes extracts from wills and many other records.

Ayscough

WALTER, J. CONWAY. *The Ayscough family and their connections ...* Horncastle: W.K. Morton, 1896. 15-18th c.

Banks

HILL, J.W.F., ed. *The letters and papers of the Banks family of Revesby Abbey, 1704-1760.* L.R.S. **45,** 1952. Includes pedigree, 17-18th c.

Bard

S., G.S. 'Pedigree of Bard of Lincolnshire, Middlesex and Bucks., and Viscount Bellamont of the Kingdom of Ireland', *Collectanea topographica et genealogica* **4,** 1837, 59-61. 16-18th c.

Bardolf

CLAY, SIR CHARLES. 'Hugh Bardolf the justice and his family', *L.H.A.* **1,** 1966, 4-28. Includes calendar of 21 12-13th c. deeds, with medieval pedigree.

Barkham

M[ASSINGBERD], W.O. 'Barkham of Wainfleet', *L.N.Q.* **4,** 1896, 80-82. 17-18th c.

OWEN, A.E.B. 'The Barkhams of Wainfleet and their estates', *L.H.* **2**(8), 1961, 1-9. 17-18th c.

Barnes

See Atkinson

Baron

'The Huguenot families in England, II: the Barons', *Ancestor* **3,** Oct. 1902, 105-17. Of Boston; includes pedigree, 16-17th c.

Beare

FARMERY, EVA. 'Craftsmen at Croft', *L.H.A.* **2,** 1967, 21-9. Notes on the account books of Joseph Beare and Joseph Proctor, including information on the Beare family, 18-19th c.

Beauclerk

ADAMSON, DONALD, & DEWAR, PETER BEAUCLERK. *The house of Nell Gwyn: the fortunes of the Beauclerk family, 1670-1974.* William Kimber, 1974. Of London, Lincolnshire and Nottinghamshire. Dukes of St.Albans.

Beavington

See Atkinson

Beelsby

MASSINGBERD, W.O. 'Beelsby of Belesby (Beelsby)', *L.N.Q.* **10,** 1909, 197-9. Medieval; includes pedigree.

Bek

MASSINGBERD, W.O. 'An account of the family of Bek, of Lusby', *A.A.S.R.P.* **24**(1), 1897, 33-56. Includes pedigree, 12-14th c., and deed abstracts, *etc.*

Beke

BEKE, CHARLES T. 'Observations on the pedigree of the family of Beke of Edresby in the County of Lincoln, *Collectanea topographica et genealogica* **4,** 1837, 331-45. 13-14th c.

Bellamont

See Bard

Beningworth

B[IRD], W.H.B. 'Beningworth of Beningworth', *Genealogist* N.S. **15,** 1899, 12-16. See also 68-70 & 140-45. Includes pedigree, 12-14th c.

Beningworth *continued*

POYNTON, E.M. 'The heirs of William Fitz Ralph and the family of Beningworth', *Genealogist* N.S. **17**, 1901, 82-9. 12-13th c.

Beresford

MADDISON, A.R. 'The Beresfords of Sudbrooke Holme', *L.N.Q.* **6**, 1901, 127-8. Includes pedigree, 18th c.

Bernard

MORIARTY, G. ANDREWS. 'Bernard of Epworth, Co.Lincoln', *New England historical and genealogical register* **113**, 1959, 189-92. 16-17th c., includes parish register extracts.

Bertie

GOFF, CECILIE. *Three generations of a loyal house.* Barnet: Rampart Lions Press, 1957. Bertie family of Grimsthorpe, 16-17th c.

Billington

WHISTON, R.N. 'Francis Billington & Lincolnshire', *New England historical and genealogical register* **124**, 1970, 116-8. Includes extracts from a survey of the manor of Spalding, 1650.

Birchall

See Atkinson

Bishop

VENN, J. 'Bishop of Hemswell: visitation of 1592', *L.N.Q.* **6**, 1901, 233-5. Includes pedigree, 16-18th c.

Blyton

BINNALL, PETER G. 'The family of Blyton', *L.H.* 1(1), 1947, 26-34. Medieval.

Bolles

See Conyers

Booth

GREENFIELD, B.W. 'Booth memoranda', *M.G.H.* N.S. **1**, 1874, 65-6. Of Market Rasen; monumental inscriptions and parish register extracts with genealogical notes, 17-18th c.

Bothamley

ASHWOOD, PETER F. 'The Bothamleys of Lincolnshire, watch and clockmakers', *L.F.H.S.M.* 4(1), 1990, 94-5. 18-20th c.

Boucherett

IMRAY, JEAN. 'The Boucherett family archives', *L.H.* 2(3), 1957, 11-23. 16-18th c.

Brackenbury

BRACKENBURY, C.E. *The Brackenburys of Lincolnshire: a sketch for a portrait of a Lincolnshire family.* Lincoln: S.L.H.A., 1983. Medieval-20th c.

Bradbury

See Whitgift

Bradfield

See Foster

Bradstreet

GREENWOOD, ISAAC J. 'Gov. Simon Bradstreet's ancestry', *New England historical and genealogical register* **48**, 1894, 168-71. Of Horbling; includes will of Simon Bradstreet, 1620.

Brakenberg

'Some notes on the family of Brakenberg', *L.N.Q.* **12**, 1912, 81-7. Medieval; includes pedigrees and notes on deeds, *etc.*

Braose

See De Albini

Breeton

See Skinner

Bristowe

See Heron

Browne

LARKEN, ARTHUR STAUNTON, & GREEN, EVERARD. 'Pedigree of the family of Browne of Horbling, Co.Lincoln', *Genealogist* **3**, 1879, 70-77. See also 191-2; **5**, 1881, 185.

SIMPSON, JUSTIN. 'Browne family of Crowland', *F.N.Q.* **2**, 1892-4, 346-8. 17th c.

MADDISON, A.R. 'A chest of useless papers', *L.N.Q.* **9**, 1907, 194-205. Browne family of Yawthorpe, 17th c.

Brownlow

See Cust

24

Burgh
C[OKAYNE], G.E. 'Pedigree of the Lords Burgh of Gainsborough', *Genealogist* N.S. 12, 1896, 233-5. 15-17th c.
WALKER, J.W. 'The Burghs of Cambridgeshire and Yorkshire, and the Watertons of Lincolnshire and Yorkshire', *Yorkshire archaeological journal* 30, 1931, 311-419. Includes pedigrees, medieval-19th c.

Burrell
FOSTER, C.W. *Burrell of Dowsby, Co.Lincoln, and of Righall, Co.Rutland.* Rotherham: Chas. M. Ratcliffe, 1885. Mainly 17-18th c.

Burton
BURTON, P.A. 'A short history of a Burton family of Sutton Bridge and District', *S.L.H.A.F.H.S.N.* 6(7), 1989, 198-200. 19-20th c.

Burtt
BURTT, MARY BOWEN. *The Burtts: a Lincolnshire Quaker family, 1500-1900.* Hull: Burtt Bros., 1937. Includes pedigree, 15-19th c.

Busfeild
See Atkinson

Butler
GREEN, EVERARD. 'Pedigree of Alban Butler and Charles Butler of the ancient family of Butler of Aston le Walls, Co.Northampton, and of Wykeham in the parish of Spalding, Co.Lincoln', *M.G.H.* 4th series 3, 1910, 73-6. 16-19th c.

Calthorpe
CARR-CALTHROP, CHRISTOPHER WILLIAM. *Notes on the family of Calthorpe & Calthrop in the counties of Norfolk and Lincolnshire ...* Chiswick Press, 1905. Medieval-19th c., includes pedigrees.

Calthrop
See Calthorpe

Caparn
HEMINGWAY, G. 'The Caparns of Lincolnshire', *S.L.H.A.F.H.S.N.* 3(1), 1983, 7-11; 3(2), 1984, 5-12. See also 4(1), 1984, 10-17; 5(1), 1985, 11; 5(3), 1986, 23. 16-20th c.

Carr(e)
C., 'Family of Carre or Carr of Sleaford', *Genealogist* 3, 1879, 193-206. See also 4, 1880, 169. 16-17th c.
C., 'Carre of Sleaford and Carre of Stackhouse', *Genealogist* 3, 1879, 380-6. Stackhouse, Yorkshire. 15-17th c.
MOORE, MAURICE P. *The family of Carre of Sleaford, Co.Lincoln.* Sleaford: William Fawcett, 1863. Includes pedigree, 16-17th c.
See also Kerr

Chapman
'Pedigree of Chapman', *M.G.H.* 4th series 2, 1908, 197. 18th c.

Cheney
MADDISON, A.R. 'The Cheney family', *L.N.Q.* 7, 1904, 150-55. Includes pedigree, 15-17th c.

Cholmeley
CHOLMELEY, GUY HARGREAVES, ed. *Letters and papers of the Cholmeleys from Wainfleet, 1813-1853.* L.R.S. 59, 1964. Includes pedigrees of Cholmeley, Waldo, Adye and Miller, 18-19th c.

Clayton
FLETCHER, W.G.D. 'The family of Clayton of Great Grimsby, Co.Lincoln', *Genealogist* N.S. 23, 1907, 80-83. 16-18th c.
JACKSON, GORDON. 'The Claytons of Grimsby: local trade and politics in the eighteenth and early nineteenth centuries', *L.H.A.* 9, 1974, 43-52.

Clipsham
G., A.H. 'Notes on visitation of Lincolnshire, 1634: Clipsham', *M.G.H.* 2nd series 3, 1890, 81-3. Pedigree, with list of wills, extracts from Walesby parish register, *etc.*

Cobeldick
COBELDICK, TREVOR M. 'The Cobeldick collection', *L.F.H.S.M.* 2(3), 1991, 100-101. General discussion of the surname.

Coke
C., G.A. 'Coke', *M.G.H.* N.S. 1, 1874, 299. Note concerning Clement Coke of Mintinge, died 1610.

COLE, JAMES EDWIN. *The genealogy of the family of Cole, in the County of Devon, and those of its branches which settled in Suffolk, Hampshire, Surrey, Lincolnshire and Ireland.* John Russell Smith, 1867. 13-19th c.

Coleville
WELBY, ALFRED C.E. 'Bytham Castle and Coleville family', *L.N.Q.* **15**, 1919, 18-26. Includes pedigree, 12-13th c.

Constable
See Heron

Conyers
'Copy of memorandum printed and bound in Breeches bible', *M.G.H.* 4th series **2**, 1908, 43-4. Conyers and Bolles families, 17th c.

Copledike
MASSINGBERD, W.O. 'Copledike of Harrington', *A.A.S.R.P.* **28**(1), 1905, 1-27. Includes pedigree, 13-16th c.

Crayle
See Heron

Creon
POYNTON, E.M. 'The fee of Creon', *Genealogist* N.S. **18**, 1902, 162-6 & 219-25. 12-13th c.

Cressy
F., W.E. 'Cressy Hall and its owners', *South Holland magazine* **2**, 1870, passim. Cressy family, medieval.
MADDISON, A.R. 'The Cressy family', *Ancestor* **9**, April 1904, 235.

Crust
WOOD, MICHAEL J. 'The upper Crusts', *Family tree magazine* **8**(5), 1992, 4-5. Crust family of Lincolnshire, 18-20th c., showing forebears of John Major and Margaret Thatcher.

Cumberland
'Family of Bishop Cumberland', *F.N.Q.* **2**, 1892-4, 277-81. 17th c.

Cust
CUST, CAROLINE. *Some account of the Cust family, from the time of Edward IV to the present day.* C.F. Roworth, 1923. Includes list of the Custs of Pinchbeck, 1479-1923.

CUST, ELIZABETH. *Records of the Cust family.* 3 vols. Mitchell and Hughes, 1894-1927. Pt.1. The Pinchbeck, Stamford, and Belton branches. Medieval-19th c., includes many deeds. Pt.2. The Brownlows of Belton, 1550-1779. Includes a 'Calendar of charters ... referring to the Gosberton property'. Pt.3. Sir John Cust P.C., M.P. for Grantham, 1742-1770, Speaker of the House of Commons, 1761-1770. [Memoirs and correspondence.]

Dalison
BOYD, W. 'Dalison notes', *M.G.H.* 2nd series **3**, 1890, 28-30, 41-3, 60, 86-8, 102-3, 122-4, 149-50, 204-5 & 232; 2nd series **4**, 1892, 187-8, 198-200, 217-8, 261-2, 275-8 & 294-5; 2nd series **5**, 1894, 139-40 & 148-52. Medieval-17th c.
'Dalison', *M.G.H.* 2nd series **2**, 1888, 40-41 & 56-7. Pedigrees, medieval-17th c.

Dalyson
DALISON, MRS. 'Dalyson and Tuthill: close rolls, 34 Elizabeth, part 8 (no.1412)', *M.G.H.* 3rd series **2**, 1898, 1-2. Marriage settlement.

Darwin
BURKE, H. FARNHAM. 'Pedigree of Darwin', *M.G.H.* 2nd series **3**, 1890, 12-21. 16-19th c.

De Albini
DUDDING, REGINALD C. 'Ludborough', *A.A.S.R.P.* **42**(2), 1937, 189-220. Includes pedigrees of De Albini, 11-13th c., Ross, 13-15th c., Braose, 13-15th c.

De La Launde
See Ashby

De Vantier
P[EET], H. 'Genealogical memoranda relating to the Huguenot family of De Vantier', *M.G.H.* 2nd series **2**, 1888, 31-2. 17-19th c. Includes extracts from the parish registers of Thorney, Cambridgeshire, and Horbling, Lincolnshire.
PEET, HENRY. 'Genealogical memoranda relating to the Huguenot family of De Vantier', *Proceedings of the Huguenot Society of London* **3**, 1888-91, 381-6. Includes pedigree, 17-19th c.
See also Wanty

Deacon

DEACON, EDWARD. *The descent of the family of Deacon of Elstowe and London, with some genealogical, biographical and topographical notes, and sketches of allied families, including Reynes of Clifton and Meres of Kirton.* Bridgeport, Connecticut: privately published, 1898. Includes pedigrees, medieval-19th c. Elstowe, Bedfordshire; Clifton Reynes, Buckinghamshire, and Kirton, Lincolnshire.

Dearman
See Atkinson

Death

B., G. 'Pedigree of Death of Stamford', *M.G.H.* 4th series 3, 1910, 321. 17th c.

Desforges

DESFORGES, ARTHUR NORMAN. 'The flight of the Huguenots', *L.F.H.S.M.* 2(1), 1991, 14-16. Desforges family, 17-19th c.

Deyncourt

B[IRD], W.H.B. 'The Kirkstead chartulary: Deyncourt', *Genealogist* N.S. **17**, 1901, 161-3. Deyncourt family pedigree, 12-14th c.

Dickenson
See Norton

Digby
See Moore

Dighton

'Dighton family', *L.N.Q.* **16**, 1921, 230-33; **17**, 1923, 83-4. See also 149-50. Includes pedigree, 17th c.
'A Lincolnshire Marsh parson in the 17th century', *L.N.Q.* **8**, 1905, 155-9. Includes pedigree of Dighton family, 16-18th c., with will of Everard Dighton of Bucknall.

Dinham

GREEN EVERARD. 'Pedigree of the family of Dinham (Dynham, Denham) of Stamford and Spalding, Co.Lincoln, descended from the family of Dinham, Co.Buckingham', *M.G.H.* 4th series **2**, 1908, 17-20. 16-19th c.

Doughty

WILLIAMS, E. 'The Doughty family', *L.N.Q.* **21**, 1931, 83-5. 17-18th c.

Dove

M., S.S.C.J. 'Dove: list of Doves in the University of Cambridge', *M.G.H.* 2nd series **1**, 1886, 166-7. Of Lincolnshire and Leicestershire; 16-19th c.

D'Oyry

MAJOR, KATHLEEN. *The D'Oyrys of South Lincolnshire, Norfolk and Holderness, 1130-1275.* Lincoln: the author, 1984. Includes pedigree.

Durrad

LANG, C.H. DURRAD. *Records of the Durrad family, 1383-1923.* Leeson & Risley, 1923. Includes many will abstracts and extracts from parish registers.

Dymoke

MADDISON, A.R. 'The Dymoke family', *L.N.Q.* **3**, 1893, 227-32; **4**, 1896, 5-7. 18th c., includes pedigree.
See also Marmion

Dynham
See Dinham

Earle

FOLJAMBE, CECIL G. SAVILLE. 'Earle family', *L.N.Q.* **3**, 1893, 94-6. See also 62.

Edwards
See Atkinson

Elsey

MYDDLETON, W.M. *Genealogical notes on the Elseys of Low Toynton, Hemingby & Bucknall, all in the County of Lincoln.* Horncastle: W.K. Morton and Sons, 1915. Includes pedigree, 17-20th c., wills, and parish register extracts.

Elwes

ELWES, DUDLEY GEORGE CARY. *An account or history of all the different branches of the Elwes family now extant in England.* Privately printed, 1866. Of Lincolnshire, Northamptonshire, Suffolk and Gloucestershire.

Esmont

ROUND, J. HORACE. 'An authoritative ancestor', *Ancestor* 1, April 1902, 189-94. Esmont family, 12th c.

Everard, etc.

GREEN, EVERARD. 'A tentative pedigree of the family of Everard, Evered, Everyd, Everett, Everitt of Kesteven and South Holland in the County of Lincoln', *M.G.H.* 4th series 3, 1910, 298-304 & 349-59. 16-19th c.

Everingham

See Heron

Evington

GREEN, EVERARD. 'Pedigree of Evington of Spalding, Co.Lincoln', *Genealogist* 2, 1878, 263-5.

Evison

EVISON, JEAN. 'Beginnings of the surname Evison', *L.F.H.S.M.* 3(3), 1992, 116-8. General discussion.

Farrer

'Farrer of Ewood, Co.York, Hoddesden, Co.Herts, and Croxton, Co.Lincs', *M.G.H.* 5th series 9, 1935-7, 224-8. Pedigree, 16-18th c.

Field

FLETCHER, W.G. DIMOCK. 'Field of Laceby and Ulceby, Co.Lincoln', *Genealogist* 2, 1878, 344-7; 5, 1881, 179-83; N.S. 1, 1884, 92-6. 17-19th c., includes extracts from parish registers, wills, inquisitions post mortem and monumental inscriptions.

Fisher

ROBINSON, GEOFFREY. *Hedingham harvest: family life in rural England.* Constable, 1977. Fisher, Maitland and Millson families, 19th c. Includes pedigrees.

Fitz Ralph

See Beningworth

Fitzwilliam

HIGGINS, ALFRED. *On an illuminated and emblazoned copy of the statutes from Edward II to Henry VI, illustrating the genealogy of the family of Fitzwilliam of Mablethorpe, Co.Lincoln.* J.B. Nichols and Sons, 1900. Medieval.

Higgins, A. 'An illuminated and emblazoned copy of the statutes of the genealogy of the family of Fitzwilliam of Mablethorpe, Lincs', *Archaeologia* 57, 1900, 1-10.

Flinders

BURNBY, J.G.L. 'The Flinders family of Donington: medical practice and family life in an eighteenth century Fenland town', *L.H.A.* 23, 1988, 51-8. Includes pedigree.

Foster

FOSTER, W.E. *Notes on the Foster family of Dowsby and Moulton, Co.Lincoln, and their marriage connections.* Mitchell Hughes and Clarke, 1907. Includes pedigree, 16-19th c., also pedigrees of Hunnings of Whaplode, Newcomen, Sanders of Weston, Bradfield of London, Tatam of Whaplode and Moulton, Matheson, Fraser, and Macpherson.

FOSTER, WILLIAM EDWARD. *The royal descents of the Fosters of Moulton and the Mathesons of Shinness & Lochalsh.* Phillimore & Co., 1912. Includes many pedigrees of related families.

'Foster of Dowsby and Moulton, Co.Lincoln', *M.G.H.* N.S. 2, 1877, 201-4. Pedigree, 17-19th c.

Fowler

FOWLER, JOSEPH THOMAS, ed. *The correspondence of William Fowler of Winterton, in the County of Lincoln.* [Durham?]: privately printed, 1907. Includes pedigree, 17-18th c., with biographical notes on family members.

Fraser

See Foster

Frotheringham

FOSTER, W.E. 'South Lincolnshire families: Frotheringham', *F.N.Q.* 5, 1901-3, 392-4. 17-18th c.

Frow

'Bible extracts (2)', *L.F.H.S.M.* 3(4), 1992, 144. Frow family, 19th c.

Fulstow

MADDISON, A.R. 'Fulstow family', *L.N.Q.* 5, 1898, 30-32. Includes brief pedigree, 15-17th c.

Fydell

GARNER, A.A. *The Fydells of Boston.* History of Boston Project. Boston: Richard Kay Publications for the History of Boston Project, 1987. Includes pedigree, 17-19th c.

Gainsborough

DODDS, J.O. *The Gainsboroughs of Aveland.* Sudbury: the author, 1986. 17th c.

Gainsford

GAINSFORD, WILLIAM DUNN. *Annals of the house of Gainsford, at sometimes of the Counties of Surrey, Oxon, Monmouth, Nottingham, Lincoln & Kent, between the years A.D. 1331 and A.D. 1909.* Horncastle: W.K. Morton & Sons, 1909. Includes pedigrees.

Gamlyn

GREEN, EVERARD. 'Pedigree of Gamlyn of Spalding, Co.Lincoln', *Genealogist* **2**, 1877, 386-7. 16-18th c.

Gant

See Irnham

Gardiner

See Moore

Garford

GARFORD, JOHN. 'Garford of Steeton Hall, Yorkshire, and Garford, of Corby, Lincolnshire: Arthur Garforth, afterwards called Garford', *N.G.* **4**, 1901, 137. 17th c.

Garthwaite

M., S.S.C.J. 'Family of Garthwaite, otherwise Gathwaite', *M.G.H.* N.S. **4**, 1884, 423-8. 16-19th c.

M., S.S.C.J., & SIMPSON, J. 'Garthwaite', *M.G.H.* 2nd series **1**, 1886, 110-11. Extracts from Fulbeck and Grantham registers, 17-18th c.

Ghent

SHERMAN, RICHARD M. *The continental origins of the Ghent family of Lincolnshire.* [ ]: Association of Friends of Bardney Abbey, [1978]. Medieval; includes pedigree.

SHERMAN, RICHARD M. 'The continental origins of the Ghent family of Lincolnshire', *Nottingham medieval studies* **22**, 1978, 23-35. Medieval; includes pedigree.

Gibbons, etc.

GIBBONS, A.W. *Gibbons family notes: a collection of memoranda relating to the Gibwen, Gubion, Guibon and various branches of the Gibbon and Gibbons families.* Army and Navy Co-operative Society, 1884. Of many counties, but especially Lincolnshire, Kent, Sussex and Staffordshire; medieval-18th c. Includes many extracts from parish registers and notes on wills, *etc.*

Gilby

See Levett

Gilliat

WALKER, ROY S. *Gilliat enterprises: the story of William Gilliat (1714-1775) and his descendants.* Buckingham: the author, 1988. Includes pedigrees.

Goche

MORTON, W. 'Goche of Alvingham Abbey (Priory)', *L.N.Q.* **4**, 1896, 109-12. See also 157-60 & 191.

Gonville

MADDISON, A.R. 'The Gonville family', *L.N.Q.* **6**, 1901, 57-9. 17-18th c., includes pedigree.

Goodhand

See Levett

Goodricke

GOODRICKE, CHARLES ALFRED, ed. *History of the Goodricke family.* Hazell Watson & Viney, 1885. Of Lincolnshire, Suffolk, Cambridgeshire, Norfolk and Yorkshire; includes pedigrees, 15-19th c.

Grantham

The genealogie of the seuerall branches of the auntient name and family of Grantham of Goltho in the Counti of Lincolne, collected from the records in the Tower, priuet euidences, monuments in churches, and other places of greate antiquite, A Dom. M.CCCCCCliii. Mitchell and Hughes [188-?]. Pedigree, medieval-17th c.

29

Grantham continued

'The genealogie of the seuerall branches of the auntientt name and family of Grantham of Goltho, in the counti of Lincolne ...', *M.G.H.* 2nd series **1**, 1886, 204-8. Medieval.

Green

'An account of the family of Green of Gunsby, Co.Lincoln', *Genealogist* **1**, 1877, 55-63. See also 395. 17-19th c. Includes list of family portraits.

Grynne

GOULDING, R.W. 'The Grynnes of Ingoldmells and East Kirkby', *L.N.Q.* **5**, 1898, 87-91. Medieval; includes deed abstracts.

Guevara

DICKINS, BRUCE. 'The Guevaras of Stenigot: Spanish squires in Tudor Lincolnshire', *Bulletin of Hispanic studies* **37**, 1960, 215-21.

Haia

GOULDING, RD. W. 'Notes on the de Haia family', *L.N.Q.* **6**, 1901, 111-5. Medieval; includes deed abstracts.

Hales

WOOF, RICHARD. 'Hales pedigree', *M.G.H.* N.S. **1**, 1874, 69-71. Of Coventry, Warwickshire, and Lincoln.

Hammond

TARRANT, M. *The Hammonds of Bassingham.* Lincoln: [the author,] 1984. Includes pedigree, 19-20th c.

Handley

HANDLEY, R.C. *The Handley family of Newark and Sleaford, U.K., and Australasia.* Merimbula: the author, 1992. Includes pedigree, 17-20th c.
HEMINGWAY, G.Y. 'The Handleys of Sleaford & Culverthorpe', *S.L.H.A.F.H.S.N.* **1**(4), 1982, 6-9. 18-20th c.

Harneis

See Levett

Harrington

MASSINGBERD, W.O. 'Harrington of Harrington', *L.N.Q.* **8**, 1905, 210-21. Includes pedigree, 13-15th c., and extracts from deeds, *etc.*

Harrison

'Harrison of Whitgift, in the West Riding of Yorkshire, and North Place, Co.Lincoln', *M.G.H.* 5th series **3**, 1918-19, 21-2. 16-19th c.

Hawksmore

POWELL, ANTHONY DYMOCK. 'The Hawksmores and kindred families of Nottinghamshire, Derbyshire and Lincolnshire in the 18th century', *Genealogists' magazine* **12**(12), 1957, 411-15.

Headworth

BAKER, LAURENCE. 'Bible extracts (3)', *L.F.H.S.M.* **4**(1), 1993, 33. Headworth family, 19-20th c.

Heneage

MADDISON, A.R., ed. 'The Heneage family', *A.A.S.R.P.* **25**(1), 1899, 36-47. Includes notes on many deeds, *etc.,* 12-18th c.

Herbert

BIRD, W.H.B. 'Herbert son of Aubri', *Genealogist* N.S. **33**, 1917, 145-51. See also 279. 11-12th c.

Heron

ROYDS, E. 'Stubton strong room, stray notes (1st series): Heron and Crayle families; endowment of a London hospital', *A.A.S.R.P.* **38**, 1927, 1-55. Includes pedigrees of Heron, 17-19th c., Everingham, Sutthill and Constable, 14-17th c., Lely, 17-19th c., Crayle, 16-18th c., and Bristowe, 17-18th c.

Hett

HETT, MARJORIE J.F. *A family history.* Horncastle: W.K. Morton & Sons, 1934. Hett family, 18-20th c.

Hewson

HEWSON, T. *A narrative of the Hewson family, ancient inhabitants of Barnoldby-le-Beck, in the County of Lincoln, with pedigrees of its different male branches, from 14th of Elizabeth, 1572, to their extinction, and to the present time, compiled from registers and other authentic family papers.* Croydon: W. Arran, 1822.

Hickman
'Pedigree of the Hickmans of Woodford, Essex and Gainsborough, Lincolnshire', *M.G.H.* 5th series **4**, 1920-22, 193-7. See also **5**, 1923-5, 312. 17th c.

Holles
HOLLES, GERVASE. *Memorials of the Holles family, 1493-1656.* ed. A.C. Wood. Camden 3rd series **55**. Royal Historical Society, 1937. Includes pedigrees.
WOOD, A.C. 'The Holles family', *Transactions of the Royal Historical Society* 4th series **19**, 1936, 145-65. Includes pedigree, 15-17th c.

Hopes
MADDISON, A.R. 'Hopes and Palfreyman families', *L.N.Q.* **6**, 1901, 118-20. 17th c.

Horsewood
HUNTER, A.W.H. 'The Horsewoods: a Lincolnshire family', *S.L.H.A.F.H.S.N.* **6**(4), 1988, 115-17. 16-17th c.

Horsman
MADDISON, A.R. 'The Horsman family', *L.N.Q.* **7**, 1904, 165-6. Extracts from family bible, 18th c.

Huddleston
HUDDLESTON, G. *The Huddlestons.* 2 vols. Bristol: St.Stephens Press, 1928. 15-20th c.

Hunnings
FOSTER, W.E. *Some notes on the families of Hunnings of South Lincolnshire, London and Suffolk.* Exeter: William Pollard, 1912. Supplement to *Genealogist,* N.S. **28-9**. Includes pedigrees, 13-19th c.
See also Foster and Newcomen

Hutton
HUTTON, ARTHUR WOLLASTON. *Some account of the family of Hutton, of Gate Burton, Lincolnshire, their ancestors and descendants.* Devizes: privately published, 1898. Includes pedigrees, 16-19th c.

Irby
IRBY, PAUL A. 'The Irbys of Lincolnshire and the Irebys of Cumberland. 3 vols. Reid Bros., 1938-9. Pt.1. The Irbys of Lincolnshire. Pt.2. The Irebys of Cumberland. Medieval-20th c. Includes folded pedigrees in separate case.

Irnham
WELBY, ALFRED C.E. 'Irnham, Painel and Gant families', *L.N.Q.* **12**, 1912, 213-21. See also 253. Includes pedigree, 11-13th c.

Johnson
GREEN, EVERARD. 'Pedigree of Johnson of Ayscough-fee Hall, Spalding, Co.Lincoln', *Genealogist* **1**, 1877, 105-15. 16-19th c.
GREEN, EVERARD. 'Pedigree of the family of Johnson of Pinchbeck, Co.Lincoln', *M.G.H.* 4th series **1**, 1906, 281-3. 17-18th c.
GREEN, EVERARD. *Johnson of Wytham-on-the-Hill, Co.Lincoln.* Mitchell and Hughes, 1875. Pedigree, 17-19th c.
GREEN, EVERARD. 'Pedigree of Johnson of Wytham-on-the-Hill, Co.Lincoln', *M.G.H.* N.S. **2**, 1877, 122-6. 16-19th c.
JOHNSON, ROBERT WINDER, & MORRIS, LAWRENCE JOHNSON. *The Johnson family and allied families of Lincolnshire, England, being the ancestry and posterity of Lawrence Johnson of Philadelphia, Pennsylvania.* Philadelphia: Dolphin Press, 1934. 16-20th c., includes folded pedigree, many will abstracts and extracts from parish registers, *etc.*
THOMPSON, PISHEY. 'The Johnson family', *New England historical and genealogical register* **8**, 1854, 358-62. Includes pedigree, 16-19th c., of Clipsham, Rutland, Pinchbeck and Spalding, Lincolnshire, Aldborough, Yorkshire, Olney, Buckinghamshire, and Milton Bryant, Bedfordshire.

Jolland
See Skinner

Joslyn
THURMAN, DOROTHY JOSLYN. 'The Joslyns: from Sempringham to Springfield', *S.L.H.A.F.H.S.N.* **6**(4), 1988, 104-5; **6**(5), 1988, 133-5. Medieval-20th c.

Kele
MASSINGBERD, W.O. 'Family of Kele', *L.N.Q.* 11, 1911, 49-53. Medieval; includes pedigree.

Kellog
UPTON, RUPERT. 'Family of Kellog', *L.N.Q.* 5, 1898, 7. Pedigree, medieval-17th c.

Kent
'Pedigree of Kent of Lincoln City (the mayoral family) and of North Hykeham, Co.Lincoln', *M.G.H.* 5th series 7, 1929-31, 177-86. 16-19th c.

Kerr
C. 'Family of Kerr and Carr', *Genealogist* 3, 1879, 88-90. 15-17th c.

Kilvington
'The Kilvington family of Saltfleetby', *L.N.Q.* 21, 1931, 70-73. Mainly 19th c.

Knight
HANSOM, J.S. 'Family notes of Knights of Lincolnshire', *Publications of the Catholic Record Society* 4, 1907, 260-66. 17-18th c.

Knowles
See Moore

Kyme
WATSON, G.W. 'The Kymes and their Parliamentary baronry', *M.G.H.* 5th series 8, 1932-4, 65-9. Medieval; also of Yorkshire.

Lafargue
PHILPOT, J.H. 'Annals of a quiet family', *Proceedings of the Huguenot Society of London* 7, 1901-4, 253-85. See also 356. Includes pedigree of Lafargue family, 17-19th c.

Lamb
GARTON, CHARLES. 'Lamb's paternal forebears', *Notes and queries* 214, 1969, 420-21. 18-19th c.

Langton
BARRON, OSWALD. 'Our oldest families, VIII: the Langtons', *Ancestor* 7, Oct. 1903, 166-9.
LANGTON, CHARLES. *The Langtons of Langton in Lincolnshire.* Jersey: J.T. Bigwood, [1930.] Medieval-19th c., includes pedigrees.

MADDISON, A.R. 'The Langton family', *L.N.Q.* 8, 1905, 5-11. Includes pedigree, 17th c.

Lanvalei
ROFFE, D.R. 'Rural manors and Stamford', *South Lincolnshire archaeology* 1, 1977, 12-13. Includes pedigree of Lanvalei, medieval.

Lekeburne
LONGLEY, T. 'Lekeburne family', *L.N.Q.* 12, 1912, 116-20 & 207-12. Medieval; includes pedigree.

Lely
See Heron

Levett
'Thomas Levett of New England ...', *L.N.Q.* 8, 1905, 241-6. Includes pedigrees showing relationships of Lincolnshire settlers in New England — Wentworth, Marbury, Bilby, Goodhand, Harneis, Levett, *etc.,* 17th c.

Lincoln
KIRK, R.E.G. 'The family of Lincoln', *Genealogist* N.S. 6, 1890, 129-39. See also 7, 1891, 62 & 178-9; 8, 1892, 1-6, 81-91 & 148-50. Includes pedigree, 12-14th c.

Lincoln, Earls of
HILL, J.W.F. 'Lincoln Castle: the constables and the guard', *A.A.S.R.P.* 40, 1930, 1-14. Includes the descent of the Earldom of Lincoln, 11-14th c.
NICHOLS, JOHN GOUGH. 'The descent of the Earldom of Lincoln', in *Memoirs illustrative of the history and antiquities of the County and City of Lincoln ...* Archaeological Institute of Great Britain and Ireland, 1850, 253-79.

Littlebury
'Littlebury pedigree', *M.G.H.* 2nd series 2, 1888, 74-5. 16-17th c.

Livesey
D[UDDING], R.C. 'Bill of complaint of Richard Livesey, 1 July 1693', *L.N.Q.* 21, 1931, 13-15. Includes pedigree of Livesey, 17th c.
LIVESEY, JOHN. 'Ancient residences in Livesey township, Blackburn', *L.N.Q.* 20, 1929, 7-12 & 35-41. Livesey family; includes pedigree, 16-17th c.

Livesey *continued*

LIVESEY, REGINALD. 'John Livesey of South Hykeham', *L.N.Q.* **21**, 1931, 98-9. Includes Livesey pedigree, 16-17th c.

LIVESEY, REGINALD. 'Notes concerning Major-General John Livesay of Hinwick Hall, Bedfordshire, sometime Colonel of the Twelfth Foot', *L.N.Q.* **12**, 1912, 44-53. Includes folded pedigree of Livesay of Stourton, Co.Lincs., 16-20th c.

L'Oste

FRANKLIN, PAULINE. 'The L'Oste family of Louth in the eighteenth century', *L.P.P.* **10/11**, 1993, 16-19.

FRANKLIN, PAULINE. 'The L'Oste family of Louth in the nineteenth century', *L.P.P.* **14**, 1993/4, 13-16.

Macpherson
See Foster

Maddison

MADDISON, A.R. 'A curious Chancery suit', *L.N.Q.* **6**, 1901, 136-42. Maddison family; includes pedigree, 17th c.

MADDISON, A.R. *A history of the Maddison family.* Lincoln: [privately printed,] 1910. Includes folded pedigree, 14-19th c.

MADDISON, A.R. 'The making and unmaking of a Lincolnshire estate', *A.A.S.R.P.* **2**(2), 1904, 337-77. Maddison family; includes pedigree, 14-19th c.

Maitland
See Fisher

Major
See Crust

Malemayne

DUDDING, REGINALD C. 'A Chancery suit pedigree', *L.N.Q.* **19**, 1928, 67-70. Malemayne pedigree, medieval.

Marbury
See Levett

Markillie

KNOX, MARY. 'The Markillies of Lincolnshire', *S.L.H.A.F.H.S.N.* **5**(6), 1986, 23-5. 17-18th c.

Marmion

BANKS, T.C. *History of the ancient noble family of Marmyun; their singular office of King's champion by the tenure of the baronial manor of Scrivelsby, in the County of Lincoln; also other dignitorial tenures ...* H.K. Causton, 1817. Includes medieval pedigree; also pedigree of Dymoke, medieval-19th c.

LODGE, SAMUEL. *Scrivelsby: the home of the champions, with some account of the Marmion and Dymoke families.* Elliot Stock, 1893. Includes pedigree, medieval-19th c.

Marris
'Marris', *M.G.H.* N.S. **2**, 1877, 248. Brief notes, 17th c.

Marshall

COCKERILL, T.J. 'Marshall of Gainsborough', *S.L.H.A.F.H.S.N.* **7**(5), 1990, 117-9. 19th c.

SPENCER, HENRIETTA MARSHALL. 'Some notes concerning the Marshalls of Theddlethorpe', *Local Historian [Lincs.]* **44-6**, 1944-5, 23-6. 17-19th c.

Massingberd

HOLDERNESS, B.A. 'The agricultural activities of the Massingberds of South Ormsby, Lincolnshire', *Midland history* **1**(3), 1972, 15-25.

MADDISON, A.R. 'Family letters in the possession of Charles Massingberd-Mundy esq., of Ormsby Hall', *A.A.S.R.P.* **23**(2), 1896, 296-314. Massingberd family.

MASSINGBERD, W.O. 'The Massingberds of Sutterton, Burnby, and Ormsby', *Ancestor* **7**, Oct. 1903, 1-14. See also **8**, Jan. 1904, 225. 12-19th c.

Matheson
See Foster

May

MAY, ALF. *Out of Grimsby.* Boston: Richard Kay, 1989. May family, 19-20th c.

Mell

PORTEOUS, J. DOUGLAS. 'Locating the place of origin of a surname', *Local historian* **17**, 1987, 391-5. Case study of the Mell surname, of Lincolnshire, Nottinghamshire and Yorkshire.

Meres
See Deacon

Miller
See Atkinson and Cholmeley

Millson
See Fisher

Moigne
MADDISON, A.R. 'Original document: from a volume of *brevia regia* issued during the episcopate of John Bokingham, Bishop of Lincoln', *Archaeological journal* **44**, 1887, 403-4. Includes pedigree of Moigne, 14-16th c.

Moore
ROYDS, EDMUND. 'Stubton strong room: stray notes (2nd series). Moore and Knowles families; two sisters', *A.A.S.R.P.* **38**, 1927, 213-312. Includes pedigrees of Moore, 17-18th c., Knowles, 17-19th c., Gardiner, 17-19th c., Digby, 18-19th c., and Steevens, 18-19th c.

More
UNSWORTH, EDNA M. 'Hugh More of Grantham and the More family', *L.H.* **2**(12), 1965, 43-5. 16-17th c.

Morkell
'Morkell of Springthorpe, &c., Co.Lincoln', *L.N.Q.* **12**, 1912, 252. Pedigree, 16-17th c.

Motley
'The Motley family in Lincolnshire', *L.F.H.S.M.* **4**(1), 1993, 23-4. 17-19th c.

Moulton
See Foster

Multon
MASSINGBERD, W.O. 'Notes on the pedigree of Multon of Frampton, Co.Lincoln', *Ancestor* **2**, July 1902, 205-7. 14th c.
WELBY, ALFRED C.E. 'Multon of Gilsland and offshoots', *L.N.Q.* **11**, 1911, 218-23. Also of Somerset and Norfolk; includes pedigree, 13-14th c.
WELBY, ALFRED C.E. 'Family of Multon of Frampton', *L.N.Q.* **11**, 1911, 209-15. Includes pedigree, 13-14th c.

WELBY, ALFRED C.E. 'Multon of Multon and Egremond', *L.N.Q.* **11**, 1911, 203-8. Includes folded pedigree, 12-14th c.
WELBY, ALFRED C.E. 'Multon of Multon and Essex', *L.N.Q.* **11**, 1911, 215-7. Includes pedigree, 13-14th c.

Neave
See Atkinson

Nevile
KENNEDY, P.A. 'The Neviles of Thorney', *L.H.* **2**(7), 1960, 23-28. 16-18th c.

Neville
CRASTER, H.H.E. 'The origin of the Nevilles of Burreth', *A.A.S.R.P.* **37**(2), 1925, 233-8. Includes medieval pedigree.
MADDISON, A.R. 'Andrew de Nevill and his family', *L.N.Q.* **10**, 1909, 142-5. Medieval.
MADDISON, A.R. 'Neville of Redbourne', *L.N.Q.* **6**, 1901, 148-55. See also **10**, 1909, 162-7. Includes medieval pedigree, deed abstracts, *etc.*
MASSINGBERD, W.O. 'Lincolnshire Nevill families', *Genealogist* N.S. **27**, 1911, 1-7. Includes pedigree, 12-15th c.
MASSINGBERD, W.O. 'Nevill families', *L.N.Q.* **10**, 1909, 23-7. See also 119. Includes pedigrees, 14-16th c.
MASSINGBERD, W.O. 'Nevill of Habrugh, Bigby and Hale', *Genealogist* N.S. **25**, 1909, 1-4. See also 143. 12-13th c., includes deeds.
NEVILL, EDMUND R. 'Nevill of Faldingworth and Snitterby', *Genealogist* N.S. **28**, 1912, 209-15. See also **29**, 1913, 64. 12-14th c.
MASSINGBERD, W.O. 'Nevill of Laceby, Sturton and Appleby, Co.Lincoln', *Genealogist* N.S. **21**, 1905, 217-21. 13-14th c., includes pedigree.

Newcomen
FLETCHER, W.G.D. 'The family of Newcomen, of Saltfleetby', *A.A.S.R.P.* **24**(1), 1897, 145-61. 13-18th c.
FOSTER, W.E. *Pedigree of the families of Newcomen and Hunnings of Co.Lincoln.* Exeter: William Pollard & Co., 1903. Reprinted from the *Genealogist* N.S. **19**, 1903, 164-9. 16-19th c.
MADDISON, PREBENDARY. 'Notes on the Newcomen family', *A.A.S.R.P.* **24**(1), 1897, 162-3.
See also Foster

Newton

FOSTER, C.W. 'Sir Isaac Newton's family', *A.A.S.R.P.* **39**, 1928, 1-62. Includes wills of Newton and Smith, and 16-17th c. pedigree of Newton.

JACKSON, CHARLES. 'Pedigree of Newton', *M.G.H.* N.S. **1**, 1874, 169-77. 16-17th c.

MARRIOTT, G.L. 'The Newtons of Skillington', *L.A.A.S.R.P.* N.S. **2**, 1940, 165-71. 17-18th c., includes parish register and will abstracts.

SILLS, GEO. 'The parentage of Sir Isaac Newton', *L.N.Q.* **7**, 1904, 126-8. See also 155-7. 17-18th c.

Genealogical memoranda relating to the family of Newton. Taylor & Co., 1871. Includes 17-19th c. pedigree, with extracts from parish registers, *etc.*

'Newton family', *M.G.H.* N.S. **1**, 1874, 191-4. Extracts from parish registers of Haydor, Westby, North Witham, South Witham and Colsterworth, Lincolnshire, and Belton, Rutland; 16-18th c.

Nicholson

NICHOLSON, S.W., & BOYDEN, BETTY. *The middling sort: the story of a Lincolnshire family, 1730-1990.* Nottingham: Betty Boyden, 1991. Includes pedigrees, 17-20th c.

Normanville

SITWELL, SIR GEORGE R. 'Gerard de Normanville', *Genealogist* N.S. **13**, 1897, 11-15. Of Yorkshire and Lincolnshire; 12-13th c.

Norton

LAYTON, W.E. 'Norton and Dickenson', *M.G.H.* 3rd series **2**, 1898, 73-7. Written notes from a printed book, 16-17th c., also of Leicestershire and Huntingdonshire.

Norwood

'Pedigree of Norwood in the parish of Spalding, Co.Lincoln', *M.G.H.* 4th series **3**, 1910, 175-6. 16-17th c.

Ogle

GREEN, EVERARD. 'Pedigree of Ogle of Pinchbeck, Co.Lincoln', *Genealogist* **1**, 1877, 270. Folded pedigree, 16-17th c.

GREEN, EVERARD. 'Notes to the pedigree of Ogle of Pinchbeck', *Genealogist* **1**, 1877, 321. See also **2**, 1878, 28.

S., T. 'Pedigree of Ogle, of Pinchbeck, Co.Lincoln', *Collectanea topographica et genealogica* **6**, 1840, 194-6. 16th c.

Oldfield

SIMPSON, JUSTIN. 'Family of Oldfield of Spalding, in the County of Lincoln', *M.G.H.* N.S. **1**, 1874, 454-5. Extracts from Uffington parish register, 17-18th c.

'Pedigree of the family of Oldfield of Spalding, Co.Lincoln', *Genealogist* **1**, 1877, 242-7. See also 278, & **5**, 1881, 123-4. 17-18th c.

Orby

GREEN, EVERARD. 'Pedigree of the family of Orby of Croyland Abbey, Co.Lincoln', *Genealogist* **3**, 1879, 271-3.

Ormsby

FULLER, J.F., ed. *Pedigree of the family of Ormesby formerly of Ormsby in Lincolnshire, now in Ireland.* Mitchell and Hughes, 1886. Medieval-19th c.

FULLER, J.F. 'Pedigree of the family of Ormsby, formerly of Ormsby in Lincolnshire; now of Ireland', *M.G.H.* 2nd series **2**, 1888, 173-9, 205-8, 219-24 & 234-5. See also **3**, 1890, 241. Medieval-19th c.

Osbert

BIRD, W.H.B. 'Osbert the sheriff', *Genealogist* N.S. **32**, 1916, 1-6, 73-83, 153-60 & 227-32. 12th c. Descent through Chamberlain, 13th c.

Painel

See Irnham

Palfreyman

See Hopes

Panton

See Skinner

Peacock

ELDER, EILEEN. 'The Peacocks of North-West Lincolnshire: collectors and recorders of Lincolnshire dialect from c.1850 to 1920', *L.H.A.* **24**, 1989, 29-39. Includes pedigree, 18-20th c.

'Note on family of Peacock of South Lincolnshire', *A.A.S.R.P.* **26**(2), 1902, 394-7. Extracts from parish registers of Potter Hanworth and South Kyme, with memorial inscriptions.

Peart
'Peart', *M.G.H.* N.S. 1, 1874, 178. 18th c.

Pepperdine
PEPPERDINE, JOHN. 'Why Pepperdine?',
L.F.H.S.M. 2(3), 1991, 90-92. General
discussion of the surname and its
origin.

Pett
LEWIS, A.S. 'Pett family, Lincolnshire', *M.G.H.*
4th series 4, 1911, 7. Pedigree, 16th c.

Phillipson
'Bible extracts (1)', *L.F.H.S.M.* 3(3), 1992, 99.
Relating to the Phillipson family, 19-20th c.

Pocklington
SANT, ANTHONY J. 'The pedigree of
Pocklington of Cumberworth, Lincs',
S.L.H.A.F.H.S.N. 6(2), 1987, 43-4.
17-20th c.

Proctor
See Beane

Pulvertaft
*Pulvertaft papers: a newsletter on the
Pulvertofts & Pulvertafts.* Newton Abbot:
D.M. Pulvertaft, 1981-. Includes many brief
articles, pedigrees, *etc.,* not otherwise noted
here.

Ransome
See Atkinson

Read
'Read family', *F.N.Q.* 7, 1907-9, 74-5. Pedigree,
18th c.

Reckitt
RECKITT, BASIL N. *The history of Reckitt and
Sons, Ltd.* A. Brown and Sons, 1951. Includes
pedigree of Reckitt, 17-20th c.

Reynardson
PHILLIPSON, MILDRED. *Holywell and the Birch
Renardsons.* S.L.H.A., F.H.S., 1981.
18-19th c.

Reynes
See Deacon

Riggall
LEARY, WILLIAM. 'The Methodist Riggalls of
Lincolnshire', *L.F.H.S.M.* 1(3), 1990, 38-40.
Includes pedigre, 18-20th c.
LEARY, WILLIAM. 'The Riggalls of
Lincolnshire', *Epworth witness* 2(2), 1971,
30-31. 18-20th c.

Ringesdune
ROUND, J.H. 'The pedigree of Ringesdune',
Genealogist N.S. 18, 1902, 216-8. 12-13th c.

Robertson
BULLOCH, J.M. 'Dame Madge Kendall's
Roberton ancestors', *Notes and queries* 163,
1932, 398-400, 418-20 & 434-7. Of York and
Lincolnshire, 18th c.

Rooke
See Atkinson

Ros
WELBY, ALFRED C.E. 'The De Ros holdings in
Denton', *L.N.Q.* 11, 1911, 2-4. Includes
medieval pedigree.

Ross
See De Albini

Ryther
See Towthby

Saint Albans
See Beauclerk

Sanders
'Saunders of Weston, Co.Lincoln', *F.N.Q.* 5,
1902-3, 190-91. Pedigree, 18-19th c.
See also Foster

Sapcote
MADDISON, A.R. 'Sapcote, or Sapcotts family',
L.N.Q. 6, 1901, 116-7. 16th c., includes
pedigree.

Sessions
See Sinclair

Sibthorp
MADDISON, ARTHUR R. *An account of the
Sibthorp family.* Lincoln: James Williamson,
1896. Of Laneham, Nottinghamshire, Lincoln
and Canwick, Lincolnshire, *etc.,* 16-19th c.,
includes pedigrees.

Simpson

MORGAN, FRANK W. 'Simpsons of Skirbeck: entries from a family bible', *S.L.H.A.F.H.S.N.* **9**, 1980, 4-6. 18th c.

Skinner

SKINNER, JOYCE, & PURCHASE, RUTH. *Growing up down-hill: growing up in Lincoln between the wars.* Boston: R. Kay, 1989. Skinner family; includes pedigrees showing connections to Breeton, Jolland, and Panton, 19-20th c.

Skinner of Bolingbroke and Thornton College, Lincolnshire. Taylor and Co., 1870. Pedigree, 16-17th c.

'Pedigree of Skynner, or Skinner, of Bolingbroke and Thornton College, Lincolnshire', *M.G.H.* N.S. **1**, 1874, 81-2. 16-17th c.

Skipwith

MORGAN, PAUL. 'Pedigree of Skipwith of Grantham and Metheringham, Lincs., 1704', *Transactions of the Woolhope Naturalists Field Club, Herefordshire* **32**, 1946-8, 55-6. Description of a heraldic roll of the 17th c.

Skynner

See Skinner

Smith

BECKWITH, IAN. 'Captain John Smith: the yeoman background', *History today* **26**, 1976, 444-51. Smith family of Willoughby, 16th c.

HUNT, ALFRED. 'A few notes concerning the founder of Lincoln Christ's Hospital (or the Old Blue Coat School), Richard Smith, 1530-1602', *A.A.S.R.P.* **35**(2), 1920, 243-6. Includes pedigree of Smith of London and Welton, Lincolnshire, 16-17th c.

LEIGHTON-BOYCE, J.A.S.L. *Smiths the bankers, 1658-1958.* National Provincial Bank, 1958. Includes folded pedigree, 17-20th c.

See also Newton

Smyth

MASSINGBERD, W.O. 'Smyth of S.Elkington', *L.N.Q.* **11**, 1911, 66-70. 15-16th c.

Snowden

MADDISON, A.R. 'The Snowden family', *L.N.Q.* **4**, 1896, 14-16. Includes pedigree, 17-18th c.

Somerford

See Atkinson

Stanley

See Atkinson

Steevens

See Moore

Stevens

ARMYTAGE, GEO. J. 'Stevens', *M.G.H.* N.S. **2**, 1877, 439. 18-19th c., also of Leicestershire.

Stone

ROBINSON, PAULINE. *The Stones of Bolingbroke in camera.* Buckingham: Quotes Ltd., 1989. 20th c. photographs.

Stubbs

BELLEWES, G.O. 'Stubbs of Stamford and Nassington', *Genealogist* N.S. **25**, 1909. 157-9. Nassington, Northamptonshire.

Sutthill

See Heron

Swan

SWAN, JOHN. *Pedigree of the Swan family.* Waterlow Bros. & Layton, 1901. 17-19th c.

Sympson

MARSHALL, GEORGE W. 'Pedigree of Sympson (of Lincoln)', *L.N.Q.* **14**, 1916-17, 190-92. 17-20th c.

Tatam

See Foster

Tateshale

B[IRD], W.H.B. 'The Kirkstead chartulary: De Tateshale', *Genealogist* N.S. **18**, 1902, 89-92. Tateshale family, 11-13th c.

Tathwell

MADDISON, A.R. 'The Tathwell family', *L.N.Q.* **7**, 1904, 179-82. Includes pedigree, 17-18th c.

Tennyson
WOOD, TOM. 'The Tennysons', *L.F.H.S.M.* 3(3), 1992, 110-12. 18-19th c.
'Pedigree of the Tennyson family', *L.N.Q.* 3, 1893, 136-7. Medieval-19th c.

Thatcher
See Crust

Thimbleby
MASSINGBERD, W.O. 'Thimbleby of Polum, *alias* Poolham', *L.N.Q.* 10, 1909, 119-21. Includes pedigree, 14-16th c.

Thistlewood
THISTLEWOOD, MICHAEL J. 'The genealogy of Arthur Thistlewood', *L.F.H.S.M.* 3(3), 1992, 120-21. 19th c.

Thompson
'The Thompsons of Messingham', *Family history* 5(33/3), N.S. 8/9, 1970, 262-9. Includes pedigree, 15-20th c.

Thorold
BURKE, H. FARNHAM. 'Pedigree of Thorold, of Marston, Co.Lincoln', *M.G.H.* 2nd series 2, 1888, 297-8. 15-17th c.
TROLLOPE, EDWARD. *The descent of the various branches of the ancient family of Thorold.* Lincoln: James Williamson, 1874. Medieval-19th c.

Toller
GREEN, EVERARD. 'Toller of Billingborough, Co.Lincoln', *Genealogist* 1, 1877, 184-91. See also 322-3. 16-19th c. pedigree.

Toppe
HULME, H. 'Pedigree of Toppe family of Algarkirk', *L.N.Q.* 14, 1916-17, 212-3. Medieval.

Tournay
MADDISON, A.R. 'The Tournays of Caenby', *A.A.S.R.P.* 29(1), 1907, 1-42. Includes pedigree, 14-18th c., deed abstracts, rentals, *etc.*
MADDISON, A.R. 'The Tournays of Caenby and Glentham', *L.N.Q.* 7, 1904, 228-37. See also 8, 1907, 242-8. Includes pedigrees.

MADDISON, A.R. 'The Tournays of Caenby and Glentham', *L.N.Q.* 11, 1911, 163-70.

Towthby
MADDISON, A.R. 'Towthby, *alias* Ryther', *L.N.Q.* 6, 1901, 188-91. Includes pedigree, 14-16th c.

Trafford
GREEN, EVERARD. 'Pedigree of Trafford of Dunton Hall, in the parish of Tydd St Mary, Co.Lincoln', *Genealogist* 2, 1878, 155-8. 16-18th c.

Treadgold
TINLEY, RUTH. *Treadgold tracery.* Lincoln: the author, 1993. Of Northamptonshire, Lincolnshire, *etc.,* includes pedigrees, 18-20th c.

Tredway
SIMPSON, J. 'Tredway family of Baston', *F.N.Q.* 3, 1895-7, 110-12. 17th c.

Trollope
TROLLOPE, EDWARD. *The family of Trollope.* Lincoln: James Williamson, 1875. 14-19th c., of Lincolnshire and Co.Durham.

Turnor
LEACH, TERENCE R. *The Turnors and their Wragby estates.* Lincoln: Association of Friends of Bardney Abbey, 1978. 17-20th c.

Tuthill
See Dalyson

Tuxworth
DENNIS, FRED. 'Finding the Tuxworths', *L.F.H.S.M.* 1(5), 1990, 114-6. 19th c.

Tyrwhitt
T[YRWITT], R.P. *Notices and remains of the family of Tyrwhitt, originally seated in Northumberland, at Tyrwhitt (or Trewhitt) afterwards in Lincolnshire, at Kettleby, Stainfield, Scotter and Cameringham, and more recently in Shropshire and Denbighshire.* Privately printed, 1865.

Upton
'Upton pedigres', *M.G.H.* 2nd series **2**, 1888, 65-8, 102-4, 113-4, 129, 161-5 & 182-4. Of various counties, including Lincolnshire; medieval-19th c.

Vavasour
'Vavasour of Belwood, Lincolnshire', *M.G.H.* **1**, 1868, 325. 16-17th c.

Veall
LANGLEY, CYNTHIA E. 'The lethal gene', *L.F.H.S.M.* 1(4), 1990, 70-72. Veall family, 18-19th c.

Ver
MASSINGBERD, W.O. 'Ver of Bottesford and Goxhill, Co.Lincoln and Sproatley, Co.York', *Genealogist* N.S. **20**, 1904, 73-7. 12th c.

Wake
KING, EDMUND. 'The origins of the Wake family: the early history of the Barony of Bourne in Lincolnshire', *Northamptonshire past and present* **5**(3), 1975, 166-76. Includes pedigree, 12th c.

Walcot
WELBY, ALFRED. 'The family of Walcot', *L.N.Q.* **20**, 1929, 87-9. Medieval.

Waldo
See Cholmeley

Walpole
GREEN, EVERARD. 'Walpole of Pinchbeck, Co.Lincoln', *Genealogist* **1**, 1877, 6-12. See also 193, & **2**, 1878, 28. Pedigree, 15-17th c.
JESSOPP, AUGUSTUS, & GREEN, EVERARD. *Walpole of Whaplode, Co.Lincoln, being a genealogy of the Whaplode branch of the family of Walpole of Houghton, Co.Norfolk.* Norwich: privately printed, 1874. Folded pedigree, 16-17th c.

Walters
ELVIN, LAURENCE. *Gab and gavel: 200 years of a family firm. Walters, auctioneers and valuers, Lincolnshire, 1790-1990.* Lincoln: Walters, 1990. Includes much information on the Walters family.

Wanty
PEET, HENRY. *Genealogical memoranda relating to the Huguenot family of de Vantier, Anglais Wanty.* Privately printed, 1902. Includes folded pedigree. Also of Cambridgeshire and Yorkshire.

Ward
WARD, JOHN CAMERON. 'My bourgeois family: an extract', *Islonian* 1(4), 1988, 18-20. Ward family, 18-19th c.

Waring
See Atkinson

Welby
Notices of the family of Welby collected from ancient records, monumental inscriptions, early wills, registers, letters and various other sources. Grantham: S. Ridge, 1842. Includes folded pedigree, 13-19th c.

Welle
LONGLEY, T. 'Welle family', *L.N.Q.* **12**, 1912, 173-4. Medieval.
MASSINGBERD, W.O. 'The Barons de Welle', *L.N.Q.* **6**, 1901, 54-7. Medieval; includes pedigree and deed abstracts.
SMITH, S.N. 'Welle or Welles, Barons Welle', *M.G.H.* 5th series **9**, 1935-7, 44-8. 13-15th c.

Wentworth
CHESTER, JOSEPH LEMUEL. 'A genealogical memoir of the Wentworth family of England from its Saxon origin in the eleventh century to the emigration of one of its representatives to New England about the year 1636', *New England historical and genealogical register* **22**, 1868, 120-39. *See also* Levett

Wesley
CLARKE, ADAM. *Memoirs of the Wesley family.* J. Kershaw, 1823. Mainly 18th c.
DOVE, JOHN. *A biographical history of the Wesley family, more particularly its earlier branches.* Hamilton Adams & Co., 1840.
EVANS, CHARLES. 'The ancestry of the Wesleys', *Notes and queries* **193**, 1948, 255-9. 15-18th c.
MASER, FREDERICK E. *The story of John Wesley's sisters, or, seven sisters in search of love.* Rutland, Vermont: Academy Books, 1988.

NEILL, NORMA. *Who was who in the Wesley family.* Isle of Axholme F.H.S., [199-]? 4 page leaflet, 18th c.

ROUTLEY, ERIK. *The musical Wesleys.* Herbert Jenkins, 1968. 18-19th c.

STEVENSON, G.J. *Memorials of the Wesley family, including biographical and historical sketches of all the members of the family for two hundred and fifty years together with a genealogical table of the Wesleys with historical notes, for more than nine hundred years.* S.W. Partridge and Co., 1876. Of Somerset, Lincolnshire, *etc.*

Weston
See Foster

Whitgift
BRADBURY, JOHN M. 'The Whitgift-Bradbury family', *New England historical and genealogical register* 23, 1869, 262-6. Includes pedigree of Whitgift, 16-17th c., and will of William Whitgift of Clavering, Essex, 1615.

Whiting
WHITING, J.R.S. 'The Whiting family', *Family history* 7(40/42); N.S. 16/18, 1973, 3-8. Of Lincolnshire, Nottinghamshire and London, *etc.*, 15-20th c.

Whittingham
DALL, CAROLINE H. 'The Whittingham genealogy and William Clarke's statement', *New England historical and genealogical register* 34, 1880, 34-7. Includes extracts from Sutterton, Lincolnshire, parish register, 16-17th c.

Wilcox
FISKE, JANE FLETCHER. 'Edward Wilcox of Lincolnshire and Rhode Island', *New England historical and genealogical register* 147, 1993, 188-91. Includes extracts from bishops' transcripts of South Elkington, Orby, Croft and North Elkington.

Wilkinson
'Pedigree of Wilkinson of Potterton', *Islonian* 4(4), 1992, 16-17. 17-19th c.

Willerton
WILLERTON, JAMES. *Extracts from the modern parish registers of St James, Louth, Lincolnshire.* Willerton family history 14. London: [], 1993.

WILLERTON, BARBARA CLAIRE, & WILLERTON, JAMES. *Extracts from the parish records of Theddlethorpe All Saints and Theddlethorpe St Helen, Lincolnshire.* Willerton family history 1. London: [ ], 1979.

WILLERTON, JAMES. *Extracts from the parish registers and bishops transcripts of Alford, Lincolnshire.* Willerton family history 13. London: [ ], 1992.

WILLERTON, JAMES, & WILLERTON, CLAIRE. *Extracts from the parish registers of Cumberworth, Lincolnshire.* Willerton family history 12. Brough: [ ], 1982.

WILLERTON, JAMES. *Willerton baptisms, marriages and burials recorded in various transcripts of Lincolnshire parish registers.* Willerton family history 2. Brough: [ ], 1981.

WILLERTON, JAMES. *Willerton births recorded in the General Register Office indexes, 1837-1977.* Willerton family history 3. Woking: [ ], 1979.

WILLERTON, JAMES. *Willerton deaths recorded in the General Register Office indexes, 1837-1977.* Willerton family history 5. Woking: [ ], 1979.

WILLERTON, JAMES. *Willerton marriages recorded in the General Register Office indexes, 1837-1977.* Willerton family history 4. Woking: [ ], 1979.

WILLERTON, JAMES. *Willerton marriages recorded in the Phillimore transcripts of Lincolnshire parish registers, marriages, vol.I to XI.* Willerton family history 6. Brough: [ ], 1980.

WILLERTON, JAMES. *Willerton references in various deposits at the Lincolnshire Archives Office.* Willerton family history 9. Brough: [], 1982.

WILLERTON, JAMES. *Willerton references in various printed works.* Willerton family history 7. Brough: [ ], 1981.

Willesbye
GREEN, EVERARD. 'Pedigree of the family of Willesbye of Spalding, Co.Lincoln', *Genealogist* 3, 1879, 138-40. 16-17th c.

Willoughby

MASSINGBERD, W.O. 'Willoughby of West Ashby', *L.N.Q.* 11, 1911, 84-7. 13-15th c.

MASSINGBERD, W.O. 'Willoughby of Willoughby, Co.Lincoln', *Genealogist* N.S. 18, 1902, 230-33. 13-14th c.

WILLOUGHBY, ELIZABETH HEATHCOTE DRUMMOND. *Chronicles of the house of Willoughby de Eresby ...* Nichols & Sons, 1896. 14-19th c., includes pedigree.

Willsop

'Pedigree of the family of Willsop of Hainton, Co.Lincoln, and of the City of Lincoln', *M.G.H.* 4th series 2, 1908, 124-6. 17-20th c.

Wimberley

WIMBERLEY, REGINALD JUSTUS, ed. *Memorials of the family of Wimberley, of South Witham, Beechfield at Ayscoughfee Hall, Lincolnshire from original papers collected by the late William Clarke Wimberley.* Revised by Douglas Wimberley. Inverness: [ ], 1893. Includes folded pedigree, 16-19th c.

Wingfield

DALE, T.C. 'Wingfield family', *F.N.Q.* 7, 1907-9, 23-4. Pedigree, 17-18th c.

Winkley

WINKLEY, WILLIAM. *Documents relating to the Winkley family.* Harrow Press, [1863]. Of Lancashire, Lincolnshire, Middlesex and various other counties. Includes wills, parish register extracts, pedigrees, *etc.,* medieval-18th c. *Additional notes on the Winckley family* were subsequently published, c.1892.

Wray

DALTON, CHARLES. *History of the Wrays of Glentworth, 1523-1852, including memoirs of the principal families with which they were connected.* 2 vols. Chapman and Hall, 1880-81. Appendix separately published 1880. Includes pedigrees, wills, parish register extracts, *etc.*

Wyche

SIMPSON, JUSTIN. 'Wyche family of Crowland and Stamford', *F.N.Q.* 2, 1892-4, 161-2 & 192-4. 16-18th c.

Wymberley

GREEN, EVERARD. 'Pedigree of the family of Wymberley of Pinchbeck, Co.Lincoln', *Genealogist* 4, 1880, 6-10. 16-17th c.

Yarburgh

'[Yarburgh family pedigree]', *L.N.Q.* 12, 1912, 174-82 & 243-51; 13, 1914, 5-8. See also 12, 1912, 206-7. 12-16th c.

Yerburgh

YERBURGH, E.R. *Some notes on our family history.* Constable & Co., 1912. Yerburgh family, medieval-19th c., also of Lancashire and Leicestershire.

Yorke

SMITH, R. GORDON. 'Yorke of Leasingham and Burton Pedwardine, Lincs., *Notes and queries,* 156, 1929, 131-2. See also 195. 17-18th c., includes inscriptions and wills.

8. PARISH REGISTERS AND OTHER RECORDS OF BIRTHS, MARRIAGES AND DEATHS

Parish registers are vital sources of information for genealogists. Original Church of England registers for Lincolnshire are listed in:

LINCOLNSHIRE ARCHIVES OFFICE. *Sources for genealogy, I: Deposited parish registers: a list of Anglican churches and registers.* Lincoln: Lincolnshire County Council Recreational Services, 1993.

For nonconformist registers, see:

LINCOLNSHIRE ARCHIVES OFFICE. *Sources for genealogy, II: deposited non-parochial registers: a list of non-parochial chapels and registers.* Lincoln: Lincolnshire County Council Recreational Services, 1993.

See also:

JOHNSON, C.P.C. 'Nonconformist registers at the Public Record Office', *S.L.H.A.F.H.S.N.* 3(3), 1984, 11-13. List.

JOHNSON, C.P.C. 'Methodist registers at Lincolnshire Archives Office', *S.L.H.A.F.H.S.N.* 10, 1981, 4-6; 12, 1981, 7-9. List.

An additional or alternative source of information on marriages are the allegation bonds required by the bishop for the issue of marriage licences. For these, see:

GIBBONS, A., ed. *Lincoln marriage licences: an abstract of the allegation bonds preserved in the registry of the Bishop of Lincoln, 1598-1628.* Mitchell & Hughes, 1888. Also indexes licences to schoolmasters and curates.

Continued by:

'Lincoln marriage licences', *N.G.* 1, 1895, 52-32, 97-102, 171-3 & 251-4; 2, 1896, 72-5, 124-7 & 164-7; 3, 1900, 9-12 & 63-71; 4, 1901, 76-81 & 140-45; 5, 1902, 35-44, 90-93 & 144-52; 6, 1903, 7-13 & 81-5. Incomplete (reached Rownthwaite) when *N.G.* ceased publication.

For a private listing of 'society' marriages and deaths, late 18th c. see:

WRIGHT, W.M. 'Note-book from Ravendale Hall belonging to the Parkinson family', *L.N.Q.* 17, 1923, 50-57.

Much work has been done, and is continuing, on locating persons who married away from their home county. An extensive listing of 'strays' is available:

Lincolnshire strays index: strays from other county records relating to Lincolnshire. 7 fiche to date. [Lincoln]: L.F.H.S., [199-].

Strays are also regularly listed in family history society journals. See, for example:

'Lincolnshire strays from Cambridgeshire', *S.L.H.A.F.H.S.N.* 1(2), 1982, 5-6; 1(3), 1982,4-5; 1(4), 1982, 9; 2(1), 1982, 10; 2(2), 1983, 7.

RATCLIFFE, RICHARD. 'Some Lincolnshire Regiment (10th Foot) marriages in Essex', *L.F.H.S.M.* 1(3), 1990, 50. Lists 9 marriages.

COLE, A. 'Suffolk strays from Lincolnshire', *Suffolk roots* 16(3), 1990, 144-5.

'Lincolnshire strays found in South Yorkshire', *S.L.H.A.F.H.S.N.* 9, 1980, 6-7. Not continued.

For Lincolnshire, many parish registers are in print. One important series is:

The publications of the Lincoln Record Society. Parish Register Section. 9 vols. 1913-25. Individual registers in this series are listed below.

Many Lincolnshire registers were also published in *Phillimore's parish register series.* The early Lincolnshire volumes in this series are indexed in:

DUDDING, REGINALD C. *Lincolnshire parish registers: marriages. Index to vols.I-VI.* Phillimore & Co., 1916.

Indexes to marriages in the late 18th and early 19th centuries are available in two series: the *Marriage index of Lincolnshire* and the *Lincolnshire marriage index series.* Publications in these series are mostly by deanery, rather than parish, and are therefore entered by the name of the deanery in the following list.

Addlethorpe

DUDDING, R.C. 'Marriages at Addlethorpe, 1561 to 1837', in DUDDING, REGINALD C., ed. *L.P.R.M.* 10; *P.P.R.S.* 204. Phillimore & Co., 1914, 1-17.

Ailby

See Rigsby

Alford

DUDDING, REGINALD CHARLES, ed. *The parish registers of Alford & Rigsby in the County of Lincoln, collated with and supplemented by the bishop's transcripts, A.D. 1538-1680.* L.R.S., P.R.S. 5, 1917. Lists signatures of clergy, churchwardens, *etc.*

Alford *continued*

DUDDING, R.C., ed. 'Marriages at Alford, 1538 to 1837', in *L.P.R.M.* 7; *P.P.R.S.* 184. Phillimore & Co., 1912, 1-61.

Anderby

DUDDING, R.C., ed. 'Marriages at Anderby, 1561 to 1837', in DUDDING, REGINALD C., ed. *L.P.R.M.* 10; *P.P.R.S.* 204. Phillimore & Co., 1914, 19-35.

Asgarby

See Nettleham

Asserby

See Bilsby

Aubourn

COLE, R.E.G., & POTTS, J., eds. 'Marriages at Aubourn, 1562 to 1837', in PHILLIMORE, W.P.W., *et al*, eds. *L.P.R.M.* 3; *P.P.R.S.* 98. Phillimore & Co., 1908, 117-26.

Aveland and Ness Deanery

MILLER, VERA E., & REED, VI. *Aveland and Ness Deanery, 1813-1837.* 2 vols. L.M.I.S. 17. L.F.H.S., 1990-92.

Barrowby

WYNNE, M.B., & ALLEN, R.C., eds. 'Marriages at Barrowby, 1538 to 1837', in BLAGG, T.M., ed. *L.P.R.M.* 11; *P.P.R.S.* 229. Phillimore, 1929, 69-97.

Bassingham

MATHEWS, W.A., ed 'Marriages at Bassingham, 1572 to 1812', in PHILLIMORE, W.P.W., & COLE, R.E.G., eds. *L.P.R.M.* 4; *P.P.R.S.* 109. Phillimore & Co., 1909, 43-62.

Beesby in the Marsh

DUDDING, R.C., ed. 'Marriages at Beesby, 1565 to 1837', in PHILLIMORE, W.P.W., & DUDDING, REGINALD C., eds. *L.P.R.M.* 7; *P.P.R.S.* 184. Phillimore & Co., 1912, 67-77.

Beltisloe Deanery

WHATMOUGH, G.W., & BARTON, IFOR. *Beltisloe Deanery, 1754-1812.* M.I.L. 6. L.F.H.S., 1991.

MILLER, VERA, & REED, VI. *Beltisloe Deanery, 1813-1837.* L.M.I.S. 6. Lincoln: S.L.H.A.F.H.S., 1987.

Belton

See Sandtoft

Bilsby

DUDDING, R.C., ed. 'Marriages at Bilsby (with Asserby and Thurlby), 1561 to 1837', in DUDDING, REGINALD C., ed. *L.P.R.M.* 10; *P.P.R.S.* 204. Phillimore & Co., 1914, 37-67.

Bolingbroke Deanery

TURNER, G.M., & WILLIAMS, I.L. *Bolingbroke Deanery, 1754-1812.* 2 vols. M.I.L. 20. L.F.H.S., 1992.

BLAKELOCK, E. DAVID, & REED, VI. *Bolingbroke Deanery, 1813-1837.* L.M.I.S. 20. Lincoln: S.L.H.A.F.H.C., 1989.

Boothby Graffoe

BLAGG, T.M., ed. 'Marriages at Boothby Graffoe, 1562 to 1837', in PHILLIMORE, W.P.W., & BLAGG, THOS. M., eds. *L.P.R.M.* 8; *P.P.R.S.* 187. Phillimore & Co., 1912, 87-98.

Boston

FOSTER, C.W., ed. *The parish registers of Boston in the County of Lincoln.* L.R.S., P.R.S. 1 & 3, 1914-15. v.1. 1557-1599. v.2. 1599-1638.

BRADLEY, K., & BARTON, I. *St.Botolph's parish church, Boston, 1754-1812.* M.I.L. 15A. L.F.H.S., 1993.

MOWBRAY, DAVID. *St.Botolph's baptism register, indexed by surname, 1800 to 1900.* 2 fiche. [Lincoln]: L.F.H.S., 1993.

HARDING, LAUNA, & REED, VI. *St.Botolph's parish church, Boston, 1813-1837.* L.M.I.S. 15A. [ ]: S.L.H.A.F.H.C., 1990.

St.Botolph's marriage registers indexed by bride, 1837 to 1900. [Boston]: L.F.H.S. Boston Group, 1992.

St.Botolph's marriage register indexed by groom, 1837 to 1900. [Boston]: L.F.H.S. Boston Group, 1992.

Boultham

COLE, CANON. 'Marriages at Boultham, 1562 to 1837', in PHILLIMORE, W.P.W., & BLAGG, THOS. M. *L.P.R.M.* 8; *P.P.R.S.* 187. Phillimore & Co., 1912, 1-16.

Bourne

FOSTER, C.W., ed. *The parish registers of Bourne in the County of Lincoln, 1562-1650.* L.R.S., P.R.S. 7. 1921. Lists signatures of clergy, churchwardens, *etc.*

43

Bracebridge

COLE, CANON, ed. 'Marriages at Bracebridge, 1562 to 1837', in PHILLIMORE, W.P.W., & BLAGG, THOS. M., eds. *L.P.R.M.* **8**; *P.P.R.S.* **187**. Phillimore & Co., 1912, 17-30.

Brocklesby

FOSTER, C.W., ed. *The parish register of Brocklesby in the County of Lincoln, 1538-1837.* Hertford: Earl of Yarborough, 1912. Includes lists of clergymen, churchwardens, sidesmen and overseers.

Calcewaith and Candleshoe Deanery

BRADLEY, K., WEST, A., & BARTON, I. *Calcewaith & Candleshoe Deanery, 1754-1812.* 2 vols. M.I.L. **8**. L.F.H.S., 1992.

MILLER, VERA, & REED, VI. *Calcewaithe & Candleshoe Deanery, 1813-1837.* L.M.I.S. **8**. Lincoln: S.L.H.A.F.H.S., 1988.

Carlton le Moorland

COLE, R.E.G., & DOLPHIN, T.W., eds. 'Marriages at Carlton-le-Moorland, 1561 to 1812', in PHILLIMORE, W.P.W., & COLE, R.E.G., eds. *L.P.R.M.* **4**; *P.P.R.S.* **109**. Phillimore & Co., 1909, 131-45.

Chapel St.Leonards
See Mumby

Claxby

DUDDING, R.C., ed. 'Marriages at Claxby, 1561 to 1837', in DUDDING, REGINALD C., ed. *L.P.R.M.* **10**; *P.P.R.S.* **204**. Phillimore & Co., 1914, 69-76.

GILLOW, JOSEPH. 'The Rev. Pierce Parry's private baptismal registers at Claxby, and Oscott, 1755-1766', *Publications of the Catholic Record Society.* **13**, 1913, 288-91.

Claypole

BLAGG, T.M., & HAMILTON, F., eds. 'Marriages at Claypole, 1538 to 1837', in PHILLIMORE, W.P.W., & BLAGG, T.M., eds. *L.P.R.M.* **6**; *P.P.R.S.* **165**. Phillimore & Co., 1912, 109-38.

Cleethorpes

A transcription of the burial registers of Cleethorpes Cemetery. 24 fiche. [Grimsby]: L.F.H.S. Great Grimsby Group, 1993. Covers 1871-1991.

Coleby

TEMPEST, MRS., & CURTOYS, W. FRANK. *The registers of Coleby, Lincolnshire, 1561-1812.* Parish Register Society **48**. 1903.

Corringham Deanery

WEST, A., & WILLIAMS, L. *Corringham Deanery, 1754-1812.* M.I.L. **21**. L.F.H.S., 1993.

BARTON, IFOR, PASK, TERESA D.M., & REED, VI. *Corringham Deanery, 1813-1837.* L.M.I.S. **21**. Lincoln: S.L.H.A.F.H.C., 1989.

Cowbit

MAPLES, ASHLEY K., ed. 'Marriages at Cowbitt, 1561 to 1837', in PHILLIMORE, W.P.W., & MAPLES, ASHLEY K., eds. *L.P.R.M.* **5**; *P.P.R.S.* **147**. Phillimore & Co., 1910, 29-58.

Croft

MADDISON, A.R. 'Gleanings from Croft register', *L.N.Q.* **8**, 1905, 195-201. General discussion; includes pedigree of Drope, 16-17th c.

Cumberworth

DUDDING, R.C., ed. 'Marriages at Cumberworth, 1561 to 1837', in DUDDING, REGINALD C., ed. *L.P.R.M.* **10**; *P.P.R.S.* **204**. Phillimore & Co., 1914, 77-86.

Dalby
See Nettleham

Denton

JEUDWINE, G.W., & GREEN, P.L.L., eds. 'Marriages at Denton, 1558 to 1837', in BLAGG, T.M., ed. *L.P.R.M.* **11**; *P.P.R.S.* **229**. Phillimore, 1921, 19-46.

Dexthorpe
See Well

Doddington

COLE, R.E.G., ed. *The registers of Dodington-Pigot, Co.Lincoln, 1562-1812.* Parish Register Society **14**. 1898. Includes monumental inscriptions.

COLE, R.E.G. 'Marriages at Doddington Pigot, 1562 to 1837', in PHILLIMORE, W.P.W., & COLE, R.E.G., eds. *L.P.R.M.* **4**; *P.P.R.S.* **109**. Phillimore & Co., 1909, 17-30.
See also Westborough

Dowsby

FOSTER, C. WILMER. 'Notes from the parish registers of Dowsby in the county of Lincoln', *M.G.H.* 2nd series **2**, 1888, 247 & 299-303. Various extracts, 17-18th c.

Dunholme

See Nettleham

Eagle

COLE, R.E.G., ed. 'Marriages at Eagle, 1588 to 1837', in PHILLIMORE, W.P.W., & COLE, R.E.G., eds. *L.P.R.M.* **4**; *P.P.R.S.* **109**. Phillimore & Co., 1909, 1-15.

East Allington

'Marriages at East Allington, 1559 to 1812', in PHILLIMORE, W.P.W., & MAPLES, ASHLEY K., eds. *L.P.R.M.* **2**; *P.P.R.S.* **70**. Phillimore & Co., 1907, 9-15.
See also Sedgebrook

East Elloe Deanery

WEST, A., & BARTON, I. *East Elloe Deanery, 1754-1812.* M.I.L. **14** & **14A**. [Lincoln]: L.F.H.S., 1993.
GANT, FRANK, & REED, VI. *East Elloe Deanery, 1813-1837.* L.M.I.S. **14**. L.F.H.S., 1990.

Farlesthorpe

DUDDING, R.C., ed. 'Marriages at Farlesthorpe, 1562 to 1837', in DUDDING, REGINALD C., ed. *L.P.R.M.* **10**; *P.P.R.S.* **204**. Phillimore & Co., 1914, 87-97.

Fleet

'Marriages at Fleet, 1656 to 1812', in PHILLIMORE, W.P.W., & MAPLES, ASHLEY K., eds. *L.P.R.M.* **2**; *P.P.R.S.* **70**. Phillimore & Co., 1907, 139-73.

Foston

BLAGG, T.M. 'Marriages at Foston, 1646 to 1657 and 1776 to 1837', in PHILLIMORE, W.P.W., & BLAGG, T.M., eds. *L.P.R.M.* **6**; *P.P.R.S.* **165**. Phillimore & Co., 1912, 65-71.
See also Long Bennington

Frodingham

ARMSTRONG, M.E., & McINTYRE, I., eds. *The parish registers of Frodingham, Lincolnshire: baptisms, burials and* marriages, 1703-1750; marriages, 1754-1812; baptisms and burials, 1807-1812. Sheffield: University of Sheffield Dept. of Extramural Studies, 1968.
ARMSTRONG, M.E., & McINTYRE, I. *The parish registers of Frodingham, Lincolnshire.* [Scunthorpe: Borough of Scunthorpe Museum and Art Gallery.] 1971. Covers 1599-1837. Includes list of churchwardens, 1751-1806.
TILLOTT, P.M., ed. *The parish registers of Frodingham, Lincolnshire: baptisms and burials, 1751-1806; marriages, 1751-1753 and 1757,* transcribed by I. McIntyre. Sheffield: University of Sheffield Dept. of Extramural Studies, 1967.

Fulstow

'Marriage index, 1813-1837 (additions)', *L.F.H.S.M.* **1**(4), 1990, 92. From Fulstow and Kirmond le Mire.

Gainsborough

FOSTER, C.W., ed. *The parish registers of Gainsborough, in the County of Lincoln.* L.R.S., P.R.S. **6**, 1920. v.1. 1564-1640. All published. Lists signatures of clergy, churchwardens, *etc.*
GURNHILL, J. *Monograph on the Gainsborough parish registers.* Elliot Stock, 1890. Cover title: *Lyffe and death Gainsburgh booke.* Discussion with many extracts; not a transcript.
WEST, A., & BARTON, I. *All Saints church, Gainsborough, 1754-1812.* M.I.L. **22**. L.F.H.S., 1993.

Glentham

See Nettleham

Graffoe Deanery

COLE, A.E., & MILLER, V.E. *Graffoe Deanery, 1754-1812.* M.I.L. **4** & **4A**. [Lincoln]: L.F.H.S., 1993.
JOHNSON, C.P.C., MILLER, VERA, & REED, VI. *Graffoe Deanery, 1813-1837.* L.M.I.S. **4**. Lincoln: S.L.H.A.F.H.S., 1985.

Grantham

FOSTER, C.W., ed. *The parish registers of Grantham in the County of Lincoln.* L.R.S., P.R.S. **4**, 1916. v.1. 1562-1632. All published.

Grantham continued

POINTER, MICHAEL, & POINTER, MARY. *St. Wulfram's parish church, Grantham, 1700-1812.* 2 vols. M.I.L. 2. L.F.H.S., 1993.

POINTER, MICHAEL, & MARY. *St. Wulfram's parish church, Grantham, 1813-1837.* L.M.I.S. 2. Lincoln: S.L.H.A.F.H.S., 1985

Grantham Deanery

MILLER, VERA, HARDING, LAUNA, & REED, VI. *Grantham & Loveden Deaneries, 1813-1837.* L.M.I.S. 18. S.L.H.A.F.H.C., 1988.

Great Gonerby

BLAGG, T.M., ed. 'Marriages at Great Gonerby, 1560 to 1837', in his *L.P.R.M.* 11; *P.P.R.S.* 229. Phillimore, 1921, 99-133.

Grimoldby

GOULDING, R.W. 'Excerpts from the Grimoldby parish registers', *L.N.Q.* 4, 1896, 112-16.

Grimsby

STEPHENSON, GEORGE SKELTON. *The register book of the parish church of Saint James, Great Grimsby, for marriages, christenings and burials, beginning in 1538 and ending in 1812.* Grimsby: Albert Gait, 1889. Includes lists of clergy, 1226-1879, and a few monumental inscriptions.
'Burials at Grimsby, 1670-1686', *Family history* 2(9), 1964, 81-6. Supplements previous title.
A transcription of the burial registrers of Grimsby Cemetery, Scartho Road burial ground. 28 fiche. [Grimsby]: L.F.H.S. Great Grimsby Group, 1994.

Grimsby and Cleethorpes Deanery

TURNER, G.M., & HARDING, LAUNA. *Grimsby & Cleethorpes Deanery, 1754-1812.* M.I.L. 1. L.F.H.S., 1991.
See also Haverstoe Deanery

Hagnaby

See Hannah

Hannah

DUDDING, R.C., ed. 'Marriages at Hannah with Hagnaby, 1560 to 1837', in PHILLIMORE, W.P.W., & DUDDING, REGINALD C., eds. *L.P.R.M.* 7; *P.P.R.S.* 184. Phillimore & Co., 1912, 79-85.

Harlaxton

JEUDWINE, G.W., ed. 'Marriages at Harlaxton, 1559 to 1837', in BLAGG, T.M., ed. *L.P.R.M.* 11; *P.P.R.S.* 229. Phillimore, 1929, 47-68.

Harmston

BLAGG, T.M., ed. 'Marriages at Harmston, 1563 to 1837', in PHILLIMORE, W.P.W., & BLAGG, THOS. M., eds. *L.P.R.M.* 8; *P.P.R.S.* 187. Phillimore & Co., 1912, 59-85.

Haverstoe Deanery

TURNER, G., FAWCETT, R., & WOOD, T. *Haverstoe Deanery, 1754-1812.* M.I.L. 9. L.F.H.S., 1991.
HARDING, LAUNA, & REED, VERA, *et al. Haverstoe, Grimsby and Cleethorpes Deaneries, 1813-1837.* L.M.I.S. 9. S.L.H.A.F.H.C., 1987.

Heckington

SUMNERS, H.T., ed. 'Marriages at Heckington, 1561 to 1837', in PHILLIMORE, W.P.W., & COLE, R.E.G., eds. *L.P.R.M.* 4; *P.P.R.S.* 109. Phillimore & Co., 1909, 73-129.

Heydour

DEEDES, GORDON F., ed. *The register of Haydor, Co.Lincoln: baptisms, burials, marriages, 1559-1649.* Parish Register Society 9. 1897. Includes list of vicars, 1559-1855, with a few inscriptions.
See also Nettleham

Hogsthorpe

DUDDING, R.C., ed. 'Marriages at Hogsthorpe, 1559 to 1837', in DUDDING, REGINALD C., ed. *L.P.R.M.* 10; *P.P.R.S.* 204. Phillimore & Co., 1914, 99-125.

Holbeach

MACDONALD, GRANT W., *The Holbeach parish register of baptisms, marriages and burials, A.D. 1606 and 1613-1641.* Lincoln: James Williamson, 1892. Includes extensive notes, a few entries from earlier and later parish registers, 1560-1788, list of landowners, 1699, etc.

Holland East Deanery

BRADLEY, K., & BASKER, S. *Holland East Deanery, 1754-1812.* M.I.L. 15. L.F.H.S., 1993.
HARDING, LAUNA, & REED, VI. *Holland East Deanery, 1813-1837.* L.M.I.S. 15. [ ]: L.F.H.S., 1990.

Holland West Deanery

WHATMOUGH, G.W. *Holland West Deanery, 1754-1812.* 2 vols. M.I.L. **16.** L.F.H.S., 1991.

BARTON, IFOR. *Holland West Deanery, 1813-1837.* L.M.I.S. **16.** [ ]: L.F.H.S., 1990.

Horbling

PEET, HENRY, ed. *The baptismal, marriage and burial registers of the parish of Horbling, in the County of Lincoln, from 1653 to 1837.* Liverpool: Thomas Brakell, 1895. Includes monumental inscriptions, list of vicars, 1222-1876, *etc.*

Horncastle

HUDSON, J. CLARE, ed. *The first register book of the parish church of Saint Mary, Horncastle, for marriages, christenings & burials, from October 29th 1559 to March 22nd 1639.* Horncastle: W.K. Morton, 1892. Includes list of clergy, 1246-1882.

HUDSON, J. CLARE, ed. *The second register book of the parish church of Saint Mary, Horncastle, for marriages, christenings & burials, from March 25th 1640 to December 6th 1883.* Horncastle: [ ], 1896.

HUDSON, J. CLARE, ed *The third register book of the parish church of Saint Mary, Horncastle, for marriages, christenings & burials, from March 26th 1684 to March 12th 1726-7.* Horncastle: W.K. Morton, 1899.

HUDSON, J. CLARE. *The fourth register book of the parish church of Saint Mary, Horncastle, for marriages and burials, from March 26th 1727 to February 12th 1738-9, and for christenings, from January 4th 1778-9 to June 2nd 1794.* Horncastle: [ ], 1908.

HUDSON, J. CLARE, ed. *The fifth register book of the parish church of Saint Mary, Horncastle, for christenings and burials, from April 1st, 1739 to December 29th, 1777, and for marriages from April 9th, 1739 to January 9th, 1754.* Horncastle: W.K. Morton & Sons, 1912.

RATCLIFFE, R.E.B., & ROBSON, E.B. *St.Mary's parish church, Horncastle, 1754-1812.* M.I.L. **19A.** L.F.H.S., 1991.

Horncastle Deanery

CLARK, B., & MILLER, V.E. *Horncastle Deanery, 1754-1812.* 2 vols., M.I.L. **19.** L.F.H.S., 1991.

BLAKELOCK, E. DAVID, WILSON, E.J., & REED, VI. *Horncastle Deanery, 1813-1837.* L.M.I.S. **19.** [ ]: L.F.H.S., 1990.

Huttoft

DUDDING, R.C., ed. 'Marriages at Huttoft, 1562 to 1837', in BLAGG, THOS. M., & DUDDING, REGINALD C., eds. *L.P.R.M.* **9**; *P.P.R.S.* **197.** Phillimore & Co., 1913, 43-67.

Ingoldmells

DUDDING, R.C., ed. 'Marriages at Ingoldmells, 1562 to 1837', in DUDDING, REGINALD C., ed. *L.P.R.M.* **10**; *P.P.R.S.* **204.** Phillimore & Co., 1914, 127.

Irby on Humber

CRISP, FREDERICK ARTHUR, ed. *The parish register of Irby-upon-Humber, Co.Lincoln.* F.A. Crisp, 1890. Covers 1558-1785, includes banns, 1763-85.

Kelstern

'Kelstern (Co.Lincoln): transcripts of the parish register', *N.G.* **6**, 1903, 90-92. 1562-90.

Kingerby

'Kingerby parish register, Co.Lincoln', *N.G.* **1**, 1895, 57-61, 115-20, 180-6 & 216-8. Bishops' transcripts, 1562-1764.

Kirmond le Mire

See Fulstow

Lafford Deanery

COLE, A.E., & MILLER, V.E. *Lafford Deanery, 1754-1812.* M.I.L. **12.** 2 vols. Lincoln: L.F.H.S., 1992.

MILLER, VERA, & REED, VI. *Lafford Deanery, 1813-1837.* L.M.I.S. **12.** S.L.H.A.F.H.C., 1988.

Lawres Deanery

WEST, A., & BARTON, I. *Lawres Deanery, 1754-1812.* M.I.L. **5.** L.F.H.S., 1992.

MILLER, VERA, & REED, VI. *Lawres Deanery, 1813-1837.* L.M.I.S. **5.** Lincoln: S.L.H.A.F.H.C., 1986.

Lincoln

FOSTER, C.W., ed. *The parish registers of the City of Lincoln: marriages, A.D. 1538-1754.* L.R.S., P.R.S. **9**. 1925.

JOHNSON, C.P.C., MILLER, VERA, & REED, VI. *Lincoln City marriages, 1754-1812.* 2 vols. L.M.I.S. **3**. Lincoln: S.L.H.A.F.H.S., 1985. Pt.A. A-L. Pt.B. M-Z.

REED, VI, & COLE, ANNE. *Lincoln City marriage index, 1813-1837.* L.M.I.S. **1**. S.L.H.A.F.H.S., 1983.

MILLER, VERA E. *Lincoln City marriages, 1813-1837.* 1 fiche. [Lincoln]: L.F.H.S., 1993. Index.

St.Margaret in the Close

FOSTER, C.W., ed. *The parish registers of St.Margaret in the Close of Lincoln, 1538-1837.* L.R.S., P.R.S. **2**. 1915.

St.Michael

MADDISON, A.R. 'Extracts from the registers of St.Michael on the Mount, Lincoln, 1575-1651', *L.N.Q.* **8**, 1905, 41-3.

St.Peter at Gowts

DUDDING, REGINALD C., ed. *The parish registers of St.Peter at Gowts, in the City of Lincoln: baptisms, 1540-1837; burials, 1538-1837; marriages, 1826-1837.* L.R.S., P.R.S. **8**. 1923.

Long Bennington

WYNNE, M.B., ed. 'Marriages at Long Bennington and Foston, 1560 to 1837', in PHILLIMORE, W.P.W., & BLAGG, T.M., eds. *L.P.R.M.* **6**; *P.P.R.S.* **165**. Phillimore & Co., 1912, 1-63.

Louthesk Deanery

COLE, A.E., MILLER, V.E., & WILSON, E.J. *Louthesk Deanery, 1754-1812.* M.I.L. **10**. 2 vols. L.F.H.S., 1992.

BLAKELOCK, E. DAVID, MILLER, VERA, & REED, VI. *Louthesk Deanery, 1813-1837.* L.M.I.S. **10**. S.L.H.A.F.H.C., 1988.

Loveden Deanery

TURNER, G., & COLE, A.E. *Loveden Deanery, 1754-1812.* M.I.L. **23**. [Lincoln]: L.F.H.S., 1992.

See also Grantham Deanery.

Mablethorpe

DUDDING, R.C., ed. 'Marriages at Mablethorpe St.Mary and St.Peter, with Stain', in BLAGG, THOS. M., & DUDDING, REGINALD C., eds. *L.P.R.M.* **9**; *P.P.R.S.* **197**. Phillimore & Co., 1913, 69-82.

Maltby le Marsh

DUDDING, R.C., ed. 'Marriages at Maltby, 1561 to 1837', in PHILLIMORE, W.P.W., & DUDDING, REGINALD C., eds. *L.P.R.M.* **7**; *P.P.R.S.* **184**. Phillimore & Co., 1912, 95-107.

Manlake Deanery

WEST, A., & BARTON, I. *Manlake Deanery, 1754-1812.* M.I.L. **18**. L.F.H.S., 1993.

BARTON, IFOR, & REED, VI. *Manlake Deanery, 1813-1837.* L.M.I.S. **22**. S.L.H.A.F.H.C., 1989.

Markby

DUDDING, R.C., ed. 'Marriages at Markby, 1558 to 1837', in PHILLIMORE, W.P.W., & DUDDING, REGINALD C., eds. *L.P.R.M.* **7**; *P.P.R.S.* **184**. Phillimore & Co., 1912, 87-93.

Market Deeping

'The plague in the Fens', *F.N.Q.* **2**, 1892-4, 153-8. Includes list of burials at Market Deeping, 1582.

Market Rasen

ENGELBACH, GEORGE FREDERICK. 'The register book of the Catholic chapel, Market Rasen, Lincolnshire, 1797-1840, with earlier entries from various sources', *Publications of the Catholic Record Society* **22**, 1921, 194-219. See also 351-2.

Moulton

MAPLES, ASHLEY K., ed. 'Marriages at Moulton, 1558 to 1837', in PHILLIMORE, W.P.W., & MAPLES, ASHLEY K., eds. *L.P.R.M.* **5**; *P.P.R.S.* **147**. Phillimore & Co., 1910, 59-138.

Mumby

DUDDING, R.C., ed. 'Marriages at Mumby, 1562 to 1837', in BLAGG, THOS. M., & DUDDING, REGINALD C., eds. *L.P.R.M.* **9**; *P.P.R.S.* **197**. Phillimore & Co., 1913, 83-112.

'Marriages at Mumby Chapel (Chapel St.Leonards), 1565 to 1692', in BLAGG, THOS. M., & DUDDING, REGINALD C., eds. *L.P.R.M.* **9**; *P.P.R.S.* **197**. Phillimore & Co., 1913, 113-6.

Navenby

BLAGG, T.M. 'Marriages at Navenby, 1562 to 1837', in PHILLIMORE, W.P.W., & BLAGG, THOS. M., eds. *L.P.R.M.* **8**; *P.P.R.S.* **187**. Phillimore & Co., 1912, 99-120.

Nettleham

MADDISON, A.R. 'Gleanings from registers and transcripts: Nettleham register', *L.N.Q.* **10**, 1909, 75-88. Also from Welton by Lincoln, Haydor, Asgarby and Stow, North Kelsey, Dalby, Dunholme, Glentham, Scamblesby and Sleaford. Many extracts.

North Kelsey

See Nettleham

North Scarle

COLE, R.E.G., ed. 'Marriages at North Scarle, 1564 to 1812', in PHILLIMORE, W.P.W., *et al,* eds. *L.P.R.M.* **3**; *P.P.R.S.* **98**. Phillimore & Co., 1908, 61-81.

Norton Disney

COLE, R.E.G., ed. 'Marriages at Norton Disney, 1578 to 1812', in PHILLIMORE, W.P.W., *et al,* eds. *L.P.R.M.* **3**; *P.P.R.S.* **98**. Phillimore & Co., 1908, 49-59.

Pinchbeck

MAPLES, A.K., ed. 'Marriages at Pinchbeck, 1560 to 1812', in PHILLIMORE, W.P.W., & MAPLES, ASHLEY K., eds. *L.P.R.M.* **2**; *P.P.R.S.* **70**. Phillimore & Co., 1907, 33-137.

Reepham

MADDISON, A.R. 'Extracts from the register of Reepham', *L.N.Q.* **9**, 1907, 164-71.

Rigsby

DUDDING, R.C., ed. 'Marriages at Rigsby with Ailby, 1620 to 1837', in PHILLIMORE, W.P.W., & DUDDING, REGINALD C., eds. *L.P.R.M.* **7**; *P.P.R.S.* **184**. Phillimore & Co., 1912, 63-6. *See also* Alford

Saleby

DUDDING, R.C., ed. 'Marriages at Saleby with Thoresthorpe, 1555 to 1837', in PHILLIMORE, W.P.W., & DUDDING, REGINALD C., eds. *L.P.R.M.* **7**; *P.P.R.S.* **184**. Phillimore & Co., 1912, 109-25.

Sandtoft

'Santoft register', *F.N.Q.* **3**, 1895-7, 323-9. Extracts from the 'French', i.e. Huguenot register, 17th c.

PEET, HENRY. 'Santoft register', *F.N.Q.* **5**, 1901-3, 116-9. Brief note.

SCOULOUDI, I. 'The registers of the Sandtoft stranger community in the parish of Belton, Lincolnshire', *Proceedings of the Huguenot Society of London* **23**(1), 1977, 59-60. Brief note.

See also above, page 10.

Scamblesby

See Nettleham

Scartho

CRAKE, ERNEST E., ed. *The parish registers of S.Giles church, Scarthoe, Lincolnshire, 1562-1837.* Lincoln: J.W. Ruddock & Sons, 1926. Includes lists of clergy, churchwardens, etc.

Scotter

AMBLER, R.W. 'Early Primitive Methodism in North-West Lincolnshire, the Scotter baptismal register, 1824-37', *Journal of the Lincolnshire Methodist History Society* **3**(5), 1982, 105-8. General discussion.

Sedgebrook

WYNNE, M.B., ed. 'Marriages at Sedgebrook (with some entries belonging to East Allington), 1559 to 1812', in PHILLIMORE, W.P.W., & MAPLES, ASHLEY K., eds. *L.P.R.M.* **2**; *P.P.R.S.* **70**. Phillimore & Co., 1907, 17-32.

Skellingthorpe

COLE, R.E.G., ed. 'Marriages at Skellingthorpe, 1563 to 1812', in PHILLIMORE, W.P.W., & COLE, R.E.G., eds. *L.P.R.M.* **4**; *P.P.R.S.* **109**. Phillimore & Co., 1909, 31-42.

Sleaford

See Nettleham

Somerby

WALKER, G.G., ed. 'Marriages at Somerby, 1562 to 1837', in BLAGG, T.M., ed. *L.P.R.M.* **11**; *P.P.R.S.* **229**. Phillimore, 1921, 135-49.

South Carlton

'Extracts from the registers of South Carlton', *L.N.Q.* **10**, 1909, 122-6. 17-18th c.

South Hykeham
COLE, R.E.G., & YOUNG, J., eds. 'Marriages at South Hykeham, 1562 to 1837', in PHILLIMORE, W.P.W., *et al*, eds. *L.P.R.M.* 3; *P.P.R.S.* 98. Phillimore & Co., 1908, 127-45.

South Kelsey
BREWSTER, H.C., ed. 'Marriages at South Kelsey, St.Mary's register, 1559 to 1812', in PHILLIMORE, W.P.W., *et al*, eds. *L.P.R.M.* 3; *P.P.R.S.* 98. Phillimore & Co., 1908, 83-100.

BREWSTER, H.C., ed. 'Marriages at South Kelsey, St.Nicholas register, 1559 to 1791', in PHILLIMORE, W.P.W., *et al*, eds. *L.P.R.M.* 3; *P.P.R.S.* 98. Phillimore & Co., 1908, 101-8.

South Ormsby
MASSINGBERD, W.O. *History of the parish of Ormsby-cum-Ketsby, in the Hundred of Hill and County of Lincoln ...* Lincoln: James Williamson, 1893. Includes extensive extracts from the parish register; also from the registers of adjoining parishes; wills of Skipwith and Massingberd families; abstracts of court rolls, *etc.*

Spalding
MAPLES, ASHLEY K., & HOWARD, W.F., eds. 'Marriages at Spalding, 1559 to 1812', in PHILLIMORE, W.P.W., & MAPLES, ASHLEY K., eds. *L.P.R.M.* 1; *P.P.R.S.* 51. Phillimore & Co., 1905, 1-193.

MILLER, VERA, & BARTON, IFOR. *St.Mary & Nicholas parish church, Spalding, 1754-1812.* M.I.L. 13A. L.F.H.S., 1992.

Stamford
TURNER, G., & BASKER, S. *Stamford churches, 1754-1812.* M.I.L. 17A. L.F.H.S., 1992.

WILSON, E.J. *Stamford churches, 1813-1837.* L.M.I.S. 17A. [ ]: L.F.H.S., 1990.

St.George
SIMPSON, JUSTIN. 'Extracts from the parish registers of St.George's, Stamford', *Reliquary* 8, 1867-8, 89-96, 151-60 & 216-23.

St.John
SIMPSON, JUSTIN. 'Extracts from the parish registers of St.John's, Stamford', *Reliquary* 20, 1879-80, 238-40; 21, 1880-81, 77-80,

157-60 & 222-4; 22, 1881-2, 53-6 & 113-8; 24, 1883-4, 73-80. Includes many biographical notices.

St.Martin
SIMPSON, JUSTIN. 'Extracts from the parish registers of St.Martin's, Stamford', *Reliquary* 12, 1871-2, 51-5 & 116; 13, 1872-3, 165-70 & 236-42. Includes many genealogical and biographical notes.

St.Mary
SIMPSON, JUSTIN. 'Extracts from the parish registers of St.Mary's, Stamford', *Reliquary* 9, 1868-9, 113-9; 10, 1869-70, 47-50; 11, 1870-71, 23-6 & 173-6.

St.Michael
SIMPSON, JUSTIN. 'Extracts from the parish registers of St.Michael's, Stamford', *Reliquary* 14, 1873-4, 41-6, 74-8 & 231-4; 15, 1874-5, 39-42, 91-4 & 170-4; 16, 1875-6, 45-8, 75-80 & 225-28; 17, 1876-7, 88-92 & 202-8; 18, 1877-8, 95-6, 149-52 & 212-6; 19, 1878-9, 46-8, 107-12 & 166-8; 20, 1879-80, 117-9. 16-18th c. Includes many biographical and genealogical notes.

Stapleford
COLE, R.E.G., & DOLPHIN, T.W., eds. 'Marriages at Stapleford, 1563 to 1809', in PHILLIMORE, W.P.W., & COLE, R.E.G., eds. *L.P.R.M.* 4; *P.P.R.S.* 109. Phillimore & Co., 1909, 147-52.

Stow
See Nettleham

Strubby
DUDDING, R.C., ed. 'Marriages at Strubby with Woodthorpe, 1558 to 1837', in PHILLIMORE, W.P.W., & DUDDING, REGINALD C., eds. *L.P.R.M.* 7; *P.P.R.S.* 184. Phillimore & Co., 1912, 127-42.

Stubton
BLAGG, T.M., & KING, R. DUNCAN, eds. 'Marriages at Stubton, 1562 to 1837', in PHILLIMORE, W.P.W., & BLAGG, T.M., eds.. *L.P.R.M.* 6; *P.P.R.S.* 165. Phillimore & Co., 1912, 139-50.

[CRISP, F.A.,] ed. *The registers of Stubton, Co.Lincoln, 1577-1628.* F.A. Crisp, 1884.

Surfleet
MAPLES, ASHLEY K., ed. 'Marriages at Surfleet, 1562 to 1812', in PHILLIMORE, W.P.W., *et al*, eds. *L.P.R.M.* **3**; *P.P.R.S.* **98**. Phillimore & Co., 1908, 1-32.

Sutton in the Marsh
DUDDING, R.C., ed. 'Marriages at Sutton-le-Marsh, 1561 to 1837', in PHILLIMORE, W.P.W., & DUDDING, REGINALD C., eds. *L.P.R.M.* **7**; *P.P.R.S.* **184**. Phillimore & Co., 1912, 143-50.

Swinderby
COLE, R.E.G., ed. 'Marriages at Swinderby', in PHILLIMORE, W.P.W., *et al*, eds. *L.P.R.M.* **3**; *P.P.R.S.* **98**. Phillimore & Co., 1908, 33-48.

Thorpe on the Hill
COLE, R.E.G., ed. 'Marriages at Thorpe on the Hill, 1563 to 1835', in PHILLIMORE, W.P.W., & COLE, R.E.G., eds. *L.P.R.M.* **4**; *P.P.R.S.* **109**. Phillimore & Co., 1909, 63-71.

Thoresthorpe
See Saleby

Thurlby
COLE, R.E.G. 'Marriages at Thurlby, 1576 to 1812', in PHILLIMORE, W.P.W., *et al*, eds. *L.P.R.M.* **3**; *P.P.R.S.* **98**. Phillimore & Co., 1908, 109-15.
See also Bilsby

Trusthorpe
DUDDING, R.C., ed. 'Marriages at Trusthorpe, 1562 to 1837', in BLAGG, THOS. M., & DUDDING, REGINALD C., eds. *L.P.R.M.* **9**; *P.P.R.S.* **197**. Phillimore & Co., 1913, 27-42.

Waddington
BLAGG, T.M., ed. 'Marriages at Waddington', in PHILLIMORE, W.P.W., & BLAGG, THOS. M., eds. *L.P.R.M.* **8**; *P.P.R.S.* **187**. Phillimore & Co., 1912, 31-58.

Well
DUDDING, R.C., ed. 'Marriages at Well with Dexthorpe, 1566 to 1837', in DUDDING, REGINALD C., ed. *L.P.R.M.* **10**; *P.P.R.S.* **204**. Phillimore & Co., 1914, 135-49.

Wellingore
BLAGG, T.M., ed. 'Marriages at Wellingore, 1602 to 1837', in PHILLIMORE, W.P.W., & BLAGG, THOS. M., eds. *L.P.R.M.* **8**; *P.P.R.S.* **187**. Phillimore & Co., 1912, 121-45.

Welton
See Nettleham

West Allington
WYNNE, M.B., ed. 'Marriages at West Allington, 1559 to 1812', in PHILLIMORE, W.P.W., & MAPLES, ASHLEY K., eds. *L.P.R.M.* **2**; *P.P.R.S.* **70**. Phillimore & Co., 1907, 1-8.

Westborough
FOOTTIT, EDWARD HALL, ed. 'Marriages at Westborough-cum-Doddington, 1564 to 1837', in PHILLIMORE, W.P.W., & BLAGG, THOS. M., eds. *L.P.R.M.* **6**; *P.P.R.S.* **165**. Phillimore & Co., 1912, 73-107.

West Deeping
'West Deeping registers', *F.N.Q.* **7**, 1907-9, 38. Brief extracts.

West Elloe Deanery
MILLER, V.E., & HARDING, L. *West Elloe Deanery, 1754-1812.* 2 vols. M.I.L. **13**. L.F.H.S., 1992.
MILLER, VERA, & HARDING, LAUNA. *West Elloe Deanery, 1813-1837.* L.M.I.S. **13**. S.L.H.A.F.H.C., 1988.

Weston
HOOSON, P.L., ed. 'Marriages at Weston St.Mary, 1562 to 1837', in PHILLIMORE, W.P.W., & MAPLES, ASHLEY K., eds. *L.P.R.M.* **5**; *P.P.R.S.* **147**. Phillimore & Co., 1910, 1-27.

Westwold Deanery
WEST, A., & BARTON, I. *Westwold Deanery, 1754-1812.* M.I.L. **7**. L.F.H.S., 1992.
MILLER, VERA, REED, VI., *et al.* *West Wold Deanery, 1813-1837.* L.M.I.S. **7**. Lincoln: S.L.H.A.F.H.C., 1987.

Wickenby
STAPLETON, A. 'Extracts from Wickenby registers', *L.N.Q.* **10**, 1909, 101-7.

Willoughby

DUDDING, R.C., ed. 'Marriages at Willoughby, 1538 to 1837', in BLAGG, THOS. M., & DUDDING, REGINALD C., eds. *L.P.R.M.* **9**; *P.P.R.S.* **197**. Phillimore & Co., 1913, 117-54.

Withern

DUDDING, R.C., ed. 'Marriages at Withern, 1560 to 1837', in BLAGG, THOS. M., & DUDDING, REGINALD C., eds. *L.P.R.M.* **9**; *P.P.R.S.* **197**. Phillimore & Co., 1913, 1-26.

Woodthorpe

See Strubby

Woolsthorpe

'Marriages at Woolsthorpe, 1562 to 1837', in BLAGG, T.M., ed. *L.P.R.M.* **11**; *P.P.R.S.* **229**. Phillimore, 1921, 1-18.

Wrangle

WEST, F. 'Infant mortality in the East Fen parishes of Leake and Wrangle', *Local population studies* **13**, 1974, 41-4. Includes list of infants baptised and buried in Wrangle, 1653-4, from the parish register.

Yarborough Deanery

TURNER, G., & BARTON, I. *Yarborough Deanery, 1754-1812.* M.I.L. **11**. 2 vols. Lincoln: L.F.H.S., 1992.

BARTON, IFOR, & REED, VI. *Yarborough Deanery, 1813-1837.* L.M.I.S. **11**. S.L.H.A.F.H.C., 1988.

9. MONUMENTAL INSCRIPTIONS

A. *General*

Monumental inscriptions are an important source of genealogical information, especially for recent centuries. Many have been transcribed; for a list of copies − now rather dated − see:

'Monumental inscriptions in Lincolnshire: deposited copies (May 1982)', *S.L.H.A.F.H.S.N.* **1**(4), 1982, 17-20.

In the seventeenth century, the antiquary Gervase Holles made many notes on his visits to Lincolnshire churches. These included transcripts of numerous inscriptions. Holles's notes have been edited in:

COLE, R.E.G., ed. *Lincolnshire church notes, made by Gervase Holles, A.D. 1634 to A.D. 1642, and edited from Harleian manuscript 6829 in the British Museum.* L.R.S. **1**, 1911. Includes folded pedigree of Holles, 16-17th c. See also:

COLE, R.E.G. 'Observations on Gervase Holles' Lincolnshire notes, 1634-1642', *A.A.S.R.P.* **31**(2), 1912, 378-420.

SIMPSON, JUSTIN. 'Heraldry in Lincolnshire churches in the time of Charles the First, from Holle's mss in the British Museum', *Reliquary* **23**, 1882-3, 29-32, 76-80 & 141-4; **24**, 1883-4, 63.

SIMPSON, JUSTIN. 'Lincolnshire church notes of the time of Charles I', *Reliquary* **9**, 1868-9, 41-8. Includes a few monumental inscriptions from various churches.

For a similar collection made in the nineteenth century, see:

MONSON, JOHN, LORD, ed. *Lincolnshire church notes made by William John Monson, F.S.A., afterwards 6th Lord Monson of Burton, 1828-1840.* L.R.S. **31**. 1936. Mainly monumental inscriptions.

An account of churches in the Holland Division, including lists of inscriptions, and notes on heraldry, *etc.*, is provided by:

[LEWIN, S.] *Lincolnshire churches: an account of the churches in the Division of Holland in the County of Lincoln.* Boston: T.N. Morton, 1843.

For tombs in the Fenland, see:

'Historical tombs in the Fenland', *F.N.Q.* **2**, 1892-4, 114-6. In Cambridgeshire and Lincolnshire.

Memorial brasses are listed in:
JEANS, G.E. *A list of the existing sepulchral brasses in Lincolnshire.* Horncastle: W.K. Morton, 1895. Supplement to *L.N.Q.* There are two supplements. See also:
JEANS, G.E. 'Lincolnshire brasses', *L.N.Q.* **7**, 1904, 147-50.
ABELL, E.I. 'Monumental brasses', *L.H.* **2**(1), 1954, 1-6; **2**(2), 1955, 1-2.
The complete brass-rubbing guide to the figure brasses in the county of Lincolnshire. South Elmham: Studio 69, [197-?] Lists brasses.
BADHAM, SALLY F. 'The Fens I series: an early fifteenth-century group of monumental brasses and incised slabs', *Journal of the British Archaeological Association* **142**, 1989, 46-62. Primarily concerned with the brasses as art.
For incised slabs, see:
GREENHILL, F.A. *Monumental incised slab in the County of Lincoln.* Newport Pagnall: Francis Coales Charitable Foundation, 1986.
An interesting general study of church monuments is provided by:
LORD, JOHN. 'Patronage and church monuments, 1660-1794: a regional study', *Church monuments* **1**(2), 1986, 95-105.
Inscriptions relating to Lincolnshire people in Australia are noted in:
HARRIS, HELEN R. 'Lincolnshire strays from Australia', *S.L.H.A.F.H.S.N.* **3**(3), 1984, 19-20.

B. *By Place*

Alford
MADDISON, A.R. 'Notes taken in the church of Alford, 19 August 1835', *L.N.Q.* **11**, 1911, 37-46. Mainly inscriptions; also includes Aswardby, Blyton, Brinkhill, Corringham, Haugham and Hibaldstow.

Alvingham
'Notes taken in the church of Alvingham, 24 Aug. 1835', *L.N.Q.* **10**, 1909, 145-6. Inscriptions.

Aswardby
See Alford

Aubourn
Monumental inscriptions, Deanery of Graffoe, II: Aubourn. Lincoln: James Williamson, [1898?] Lists over 100 inscriptions.

Bardney
BRAKSPEAR, HAROLD. 'Bardney Abbey', *Archaeological journal* **79**, 1922, 1-92. Includes many monumental inscriptions, 13-16th c., with survey, 16th c., giving names of tenants.
FOWLER, J.T. 'Tombstone inscriptions from Bardney Abbey', *A.A.S.R.P.* **32**(2), 1914, 403-10.

Barrow on Humber
'Notes taken in the church of Barrow, 2nd September 1835', *L.N.Q.* **10**, 1909, 146-50. Inscriptions.

Barton on Humber. St.Peter
'Notes taken in the church of Barton St.Peter, 1 Sept., 1835', *L.N.Q.* **10**, 1909, 180-9. Inscriptions.

Beesby in the Marsh
'Notes taken in the church of Beesby', *L.N.Q.* **10**, 1909, 202-10. Inscriptions; also from Burwell, North Cockerington, Covenham St.Bartholomew, Covenham St.Mary, Cowbit, Elsham, Goxhill, Grainsby and Haugh.

Blyton
See Alford

Boston
BLOXAM, M.H. 'Sepulchral monuments and effigies in Boston church, Lincolnshire', *A.A.S.R.P.* **10**(2), 1870, 219-23.
WHEELDON, JEREMY. *The monumental brasses in Saint Botolph's church, Boston.* History of Boston Project **9**. Boston: Richard Kay Publications, 1973. Primarily concerned with monumental art.
'An account of Boston, in Lincolnshire, with the monumental inscriptions', *Topographer* **2**, 1890, 298-305.

Brigg
A transcript of the monumental inscriptions to be found in the cemetery, on the war memorial, and in the church of St.John the Evangelist at Brigg, Lincolnshire. 3 fiche. [Grimsby]: L.F.H.S., Great Grimsby Group, 1992.

Brinkhill
See Alford

Burwell
See Beesby in the Marsh

Caistor
'Monumental inscriptions in Castor church, Lincolnshire, from Gervase Holles's mss. coll. in Bibl. Harl. Brit. Mus. Castor. A.1629', Topographer 2, 1790, 43-4.

Cleethorpes
A transcript of the monumental inscriptions to be found in the cemetery at Cleethorpes. 7 fiche. [Grimsby]: L.F.H.S., Great Grimsby Group, 1994.

Cockerington
HOLLES, GERVASE. 'Church notes from Cokerington, Lincolnshire', Topographer 3, 1790, 181-5. Includes monumental inscriptions.

Corby
See Irnham

Corringham
See Alford

Covenham. St.Bartholomew
See Beesby in the Marsh

Covenham. St.Mary
See Beesby in the Marsh

Cowbit
See Beesby in the Marsh

Croft
See Welton

Crowland
SIMPSON, JUSTIN. 'Notes on Croyland, no.2', F.N.Q. 1, 1889-91, 111-13. Heraldic notes.

Doddington
C[OLE], R.E.G. Monumental inscriptions, Deanery of Graffoe, I: Doddington. Lincoln: James Williamson, 1898.

East Keal
MADDISON, A.R. 'Notes taken in the church of East Keal, 14 August 1834', L.N.Q. 11, 1911, 87-94. Inscriptions. Also from Laceby, Lutton, Stickney and Stickford.

Elsham
See Beesby in the Marsh

Fulstow
'Notes taken in the church of Fulstow', L.N.Q. 11, 1911, 196-202. Inscriptions; also includes Theddlethorpe and Tathwell.

Frodingham
See Spalding

Goxhill
See Beesby in the Marsh

Grainsby
See Beesby in the Marsh

Grimsby
'History and ancient description of Grimsby Magna in Lincolnshire', Topographer 1, 1789, 243-56. Includes monumental inscriptions.

Hainton
See Witham on the Hill

Halton Holgate
See Harrington

Harrington
MADDISON, A.R. 'Notes taken in the church of Harrington, 17 August 1835', L.N.Q. 11, 1911, 105-12. Inscriptions; also from Halton Holgate and Redbourne.
'Church notes at Harrington in Lincolnshire', Topographer 4, 1791, 178-83. Mainly monumental inscriptions.

Haugh
See Beesby in the Marsh

Haugham
See Alford

Hibaldstow
See Alford

Holbeach
M., J. 'Church inscriptions in the Hundred of Elloe', *F.N.Q.* **7**, 1907-9, 224-6, 252-5, 281-5, 317-21, 337-41 & 371-4. Mainly Holbeach; also Long Sutton.

Irnham
'Church notes for Irnham and Corby, in Lincolnshire, and St.Columbe in Cornwall', *Topographer* **5**, 1821, 11-13.

Kelstern
See Welton

Lincoln Cathedral
BLOXAM, MATTHEW HOLBECHE. 'On the tombs in Lincoln Cathedral', *A.A.S.R.P.* **18**(2), 1886, 103-10.
LINCOLN, PRECENTOR OF. 'The memorial slabs formerly in the cloisters of Lincoln Minster', *A.A.S.R.P.* **21**(2), 1892, 190-4. Notes on 42 slabs.
SANDERSON, ROBERT. *Lincoln Cathedral: an exact copy of all the ancient monumental inscriptions there, as they stood in 1641* ... [ed.] F. Peck. Simpkin Marshall & Co., 1851.
'Lincoln Cathedral', *Transactions of the Monumental Brass Society* **2**(8), 1897, 314-26. Artistic description of 107 memorials; includes some genealogical information.
'A short dissertation upon the monuments at the upper end of the north-eastern part of the Presbytery (or choir of angels) in the Cathedral of Lincoln', in *Memoirs illustrative of the history and antiquities of the County and City of Lincoln, communicated to the annual meeting of the Archaeological Institute of Great Britain and Ireland, held at Lincoln, July 1848* ... The Institute, 1850, 241-7. Includes pedigree of Burghersh, medieval.

Lincoln. St.Martin
MADDISON, A.R. 'Inscriptions on gravestones in St.Martins churchyard, Lincoln', *L.N.Q.* **9**, 1907, 157-60.
MADDISON, A.R. 'Notes taken in the church of St.Martins, Lincoln, 7 Aug 1833', *L.N.Q.* **12**, 1912, 17-26. Inscriptions; also includes Thurlby and Louth.

Long Sutton
See Holbeach

Louth
GOULDING, RD. W. *The epitaphs in St.Mary's churchyard, Louth*. Louth: Goulding & Son, 1921.
'Short account of Louth in Lincolnshire, with church notes from Gervase Holle's ms.', *Topographer* **4**, 1791, 161-5. Mainly monumental inscriptions.
See also Lincoln. St.Martin

Ludborough
'Notes taken in the church of Ludborough, 1835', *L.N.Q.* **10**, 1909, 232-40. Inscriptions; also from Mablethorpe, South Ormsby, Rigsby, Sausthorpe, Stenigot, Strubby, Swaby and Swinhope.

Mablethorpe
See Ludborough

Market Rasen
A transcript of the monumental inscriptions to be found in the cemetery, on the war memorial and the Wesleyan Chapel burial ground at Market Rasen, Lincolnshire. 2 fiche. [Grimsby]: L.F.H.S., Great Grimsby Group, 1993.

Marsh Chapel
See Welton

North Cockerington
See Beesby in the Marsh

North Thoresby
M[ADDISON], A.R. 'Notes taken in the church of North Thoresby, 1835', *L.N.Q.* **11**, 1911, 17-19. Includes inscriptions.

Norton Disney
SANDERSON, H.K.ST.J. 'Norton Disney, Linc', *Transactions of the Monumental Brass Society* **2**, 1892-6, 216-23. List of brasses.

Rand
'Notes on monuments at Rand, April 6, 1832', *L.N.Q.* **19**, 1928, 113-22.

Redbourne
See Harrington

Rigsby
See Ludborough

Roughton
'Monumental inscriptions at Roughton, near Horncastle', *Genealogist* **7**, 1883, 171.

Sausthorpe
See Ludborough

Saxby
HOLLES, GERVASE. 'Church notes from Saxby in Lincolnshire', *Topographer* **3**, 1790, 279-82.

Scotter
MADDISON, A.R. 'Notes taken in the church of Scotter', *L.N.Q.* **11**, 1911, 138-46. Inscriptions; also includes Scotton, Sibsey and Swineshead.

Scotton
See Scotter

Sedgebrook
'Some account of Sedgebrook, in Lincolnshire, from ancient mss', *Topographer* **2**, 1790, 295-8. Mainly monumental inscriptions.

Sibsey
See Scotter

Skegness
See Welton

South Elkington
See Welton

South Ormsby
See Ludborough

Spalding
JEANS, G.E. 'Notes taken in the church of Spalding, Aug 10th 1835', *L.N.Q.* **11**, 1911, 170-80. Inscriptions; also from Frodingham, and Spilsby. For Frodingham, see also 195.
REDSHAW, E.J. 'The Spalding hatchments', *Coat of arms* **9**, 1966-7, 60-65.

Spilsby
TROLLOPE, EDWARD. 'St.James's church, Spilsby', *A.A.S.R.P.* **8**(1), 1865, 1-37. Mainly concerned with monuments of Willoughby and Bertie families.

'Monumental inscriptions in Spilesby church ...', *Topographer* **1**, 1789, 344-51.
See also Spalding

Stallingborough
'Church notes from Stallingborough in Lincolnshire', *Topographer* **4**, 1791, 238-42. Includes notes on heraldry.

Stenigot
See Ludborough

Strubby
See Ludborough

Surfleet
BEALBY, J.T. 'Monumental inscriptions at Surfleet', *F.N.Q.* **3**, 1895-7, 380-83.

Swaby
See Ludborough

Swineshead
See Scotter

Swinhope
See Ludborough

Tathwell
See Fulstow

Tetney
See Welton

Theddlethorpe
See Fulstow

Thurlby
See Lincoln. St.Martin

Uffington
SIMPSON, JUSTIN. 'Some account of the village of Uffington, county of Lincoln, its church, and monuments therein, &c., &c', *Reliquary* **6**, 1865-6, 220-3; **7**, 1866-7, 72-7. See also **7**, 1866-7, 126-7. Includes monumental inscriptions.

Welby
WELBY, ALFRED C.E. 'Ancient incised tomb in Welby churchyard', *L.N.Q.* **11**, 1911, 193-5.

Welton
MADDISON, A.R. 'Notes taken in the church of Welton by Louth, 14 August 1833', *L.N.Q.* 11, 1911, 229. Inscriptions; also includes Marsh Chapel, Kelstern, Croft, South Elkington, Skegness and Tetney.

Whaplode
FOSTER, SIR WILLIAM EDWARD. *The parish church of Saint Mary, Whaplode in the County of Lincoln.* Elliot Stock, 1889. Includes list of inscriptions, list of clergy, extracts from the registers concerning Welby family, hearth tax 1665, *etc.*

Witham on the Hill
MADDISON, A.R. 'Notes taken in the church of Witham on the Hill, 20 July 1833', *L.N.Q.* 12, 1912, 36-44. Inscriptions; also includes some from Hainton.

Wroot
'Some inscriptions from Wroot parish church', *Islonian* 4(1), 1992, 30.

C. *By Surname*

Anderson
A description of the mausoleum in Brocklesby Park, Lincolnshire, to which is added the genealogy of the Andersons and Pelhams, ancestors of the noble family of Yarborough. Louth: J. & J. Jackson, 1832.

Armyn
WALKER, GILBERT G. 'The Armyn monument at Lenton', *L.N.Q.* 14, 1916-17, 97-104. 1598; much heraldic information.

Ayscough
HAWKESBURY, LORD. 'The Ayscough monuments at Stallingborough, Co.Lincoln', *N.G.* 2, 1896, 43-4.

Blyth
WELBY, ALFRED C.E. 'Two monuments in Denton church', *L.N.Q.* 9, 1907, 225-9. To John Blyth, 1602, and Richard Welby, 1714.

Bolle
S[YMPSON], E.M. 'Monument of Charles Bolle of Haugh in Haugh Church, near Alford', *L.N.Q.* 7, 1904, 33-5.

Burnaby
See Monson

Buslingthorpe
SANSOM, JOHN. 'Notes on the Buslingthorpe brass', *Transactions of the Historic Society of Lancashire and Cheshire* 10, 1858, 203-6. Tomb of Sir Richard de Buslingthorpe, 1280.

Colby
COULBY, TED. 'The Colby memorials at Kirton-in-Holland', *S.L.H.A.F.H.S.N.* 5(4), 1986, 6-9; 5(5), 1986, 3-8. Includes pedigree, 16-18th c.

Copuldyk
SURRY, NIGEL. 'Re-dating the brass to Margaret Copuldyk, Harrington, Lincolnshire', *Transactions of the Monumental Brass Society* 10(4), 1966, 259-61. Late 15th c.

Cromwell
JEANS, G.E. 'Brass of Ralph Lord Treasurer Cromwell and his wife, 1455-6', *L.N.Q.* 3, 1893, 193-6. See also 224.

D'Eyncourt
'Ancient inscription to the memory of William D'Eyncourt, who died in the reign of King William Rufus', in *Memoirs illustrative of the history and antiquities of the County and City of Lincoln* ... Archaeological Institute of Great Britain and Ireland, 1850, 248-52.

Disney
SANDERSON, H.K.ST.J. 'Norton Disney, Linc', *Transactions of the Monumental Brass Society* 2(4), 1895, 216-223. See also 2(5), 1896, 301-2. Disney family brasses; includes medieval pedigree.

Effard
C[OLE], R.E.G. 'Tomb of Master Peter Effard, in St.Peter in Eastgate church', *L.N.Q.* 13, 1914, 210-12.

Hardreshull
DUDDING, REGINALD C. 'The monument of Sir William Hardreshull', *L.N.Q.* 10, 1909, 33-8. Includes medieval pedigree.

Heron
'Heron family of Cressy Hall', *F.N.Q.* **3**, 1895-7, 225-8. See also 262-3. In the parish of Surfleet. Monumental inscriptions.

Littlebury
'Littlebury effigy at Holbeach', *F.N.Q.* **6**, 1904-6, 380-82. Tomb of Sir Humphrey Littlebury, c.13th c.

Monson
GIBBONS, G.S. 'Unrecorded brasses: Claxby near Market Rasen', *L.N.Q.* **19**, 1928, 49-51. To Mary Monson, 1638, and Jane Burnaby, 1653.

Pelham
See Anderson

St.Paule
S[YMPSON], E.M. 'Monuments of the St.Paule family in St.Lawrence's church, Snarford', *L.N.Q.* **7**, 1904, 1-3. 16th c.

Sothill
THORPE, MISS. 'The Sothill tomb in Redbourne church, near Kirton-in-Lindsey, Lincolnshire', *Reliquary* **15**, 1874-5, 154. Medieval.

Welby
See Blyth

Willoughby
NOTTINGHAM, BISHOP OF. 'Grimsthorpe and the Willoughby monuments in Edenham church', *A.A.S.R.P.* **20**(1), 1889, 19-24. Includes genealogical notes on Willoughby family.

10. PROBATE RECORDS AND INQUISITIONS POST MORTEM

Probate records – wills, inventories, administration bonds, *etc.* – are invaluable sources of genealogical information. Wills normally list all living children; other relatives are often mentioned, as are places with which the testator has been associated. For brief general discussions of Lincolnshire wills, see:

KERSHAW, BOB R. 'Ordinary people? – plenty of wills', *L.F.H.S.M.* 3(4), 1992, 146-50.

COPPEL, STEPHEN. 'Willmaking on the death bed', *Local population studies* **40**, 1988, 37-45. Based on wills of Leverton and Grantham.

MADDISON, A.R. 'Domestic life in the sixteenth and seventeenth centuries, illustrated by wills in the Registry at Lincoln', *A.A.S.R.P.* 17(1), 1883, 21-30.

MADDISON, A.R. 'Preambles and bequests in wills of the 17th century', *L.N.Q.* **7**, 1904, 214-21. Brief note on many wills and inventories.

Lincolnshire was in the Diocese of Lincoln and Province of Canterbury. Most wills were proved in the Diocesan Consistory Court. For indexes to probate records from this and a few other courts, see:

FOSTER, C.W., ed. *Calendars of Lincoln wills.* 2 vols. Index Library **28** & **41**. British Record Society, 1902-10. v.1. 1320-1600 (from the bishops registers, 1320-1547, the Episcopal Registry, 1489-1588, and the Consistory Court, 1506-1600). v.2. Consistory Court wills, 1601-1652.

FOSTER, C.W., ed. *Calendars of administrations in the Consistory Court of Lincoln, A.D. 1540-1659.* Index Library **52**. British Record Society, 1921. Also issued as L.R.S. **16**, 1918. Indexes grants of administration in the Commissary's court and the court of the Archdeacon of Lincoln, as well as in the Consistory Court.

FOSTER, C.W., ed. *Calendars of wills and administrations at Lincoln, (volume 4). Archdeaconry of Stow, peculiar courts, and miscellaneous courts.* Index Library **57**. British Record Society, 1930.

HAINS, GRACE, & FOSTER, C.W., eds. *Index of Lincoln Consistory Court wills and inventories, 1660-1700.* Index Library **101**. British Record Society, 1991. Alternative title: *Wills and inventories at Lincoln, volume 5.* Cover title: *Lincoln wills, vol. V: 1660-1700.*

A further volume in preparation will cover Consistory Court administrations and administration accounts, 17th c., Dean and Chapter probate records, 1305-1534, and probate records of the Lincoln borough court, 1305-75.

For wills proved in the Court of the Dean and Chapter of Lincoln Cathedral, 1534-1780, and in the Consistory Court, 1506-31, see the work by Gibbons listed in section 4.

For wills proved in the peculiar courts of Caistor, 1636-1833, and Louth, 1659-1837, see: 'Wills and administrations in the peculiar courts at Lincoln', *N.G.* **1**, 1895, 42-5, 80-87 & 162-4; **2**, 1896, 172-5.

An index to a record searcher's collection of will abstracts is printed in: 'Wills and admons. etc., listings taken from Cals. of old Diocese of York and Diocese of Lincoln', *Family history* **2**(7), 1963, 7-8; **2**(9), 1964, 90-92; **2**(10), 1964, 103-5; **3**(13), 1965, 29-32.

For wills proved at provincial level, in the Prerogative Court of Canterbury, reference must be made to the many indexes listed in my *English genealogy: an introductory bibliography.* See also:

FOSTER, C.W. 'Lincolnshire wills proved in the Prerogative Court of Canterbury', *A.A.S.R.P.* **41**(1), 1934, 61-114; **41**(2), 1935, 179-218. 1384-1490.

SMITH, W.H. 'An analytical calendar of Lincoln wills proved in the Prerogative Court of Canterbury', *N.G.* **1**, 1895, 211-5; **2**, 1896, 23-6, 59-62, 131-4 & 195-7; **3**, 1900, 132-7; **4**, 1901, 22-7; **5**, 1902, 109-15; **6**, 1903, 23-30. 16th c.

The beneficiaries of wills are usually ignored in indexing. Lincoln Family History Society members have, however, cooperated to produce:

BAKER, PAM. *Wills beneficiary index ...* 3 fiche. [Lincoln]: L.F.H.S., 1991. Compiled from information sent in by members.

A number of collections of will abstracts have been published. These include:

FOSTER, C.W., ed. *Lincoln wills registered in the District Probate Registry at Lincoln.* 3 vols. L.R.S. **5, 10** & **24**. 1914-30. v.1. 1271-1526. v.2. 1505-30. v.3. 1530-32.

GIBBONS, ALFRED. *Early Lincoln wills: an abstract of all the wills & administrations recorded in the episcopal registers of the old Diocese of Lincoln, 1280-1547, comprising the counties of Lincoln, Rutland, Northampton, Huntingdon, Bedford, Buckingham, Oxford, Leicester and Hertford.* Lincoln: James Williamson, 1888.

MADDISON, A.R. *Lincolnshire wills: 1st series, A.D. 1500-1600.* Lincoln: James Williamson, 1888.

MADDISON, A.R. *Lincolnshire wills: second series, A.D. 1600-1617...* Lincoln: James Williamson, 1891.

FOSTER, C.W., ed. *Abstracts of Lincolnshire wills proved in the Prerogative Court of Canterbury.* Supplement to *L.N.Q.* **17-23**. Horncastle: W.K. Morton & Sons, 1922-35. Incomplete.

SANBORN, VICTOR CHANNING. 'The Lincolnshire origin of some Exeter settlers', *New England historical and genealogical register* **68**, 1914, 64-80. Wills and parish register extracts of the Cram, Dearborn, Rabone or Haborne, Wheelwright, Wight, Willick and Bellingham families, 16-17th c.

A number of collections of will abstracts relate to particular places:

Allington

PASK, B.M. *Allington wills and inventories.* Newark: privately published, 1989. 16-18th c.

Clee

AMBLER, R.W., WATKINSON, B. & WATKINSON, L., eds. *Farmers and fishermen: the probate inventories of the ancient parish of Clee, South Humberside, 1536-1742.* Hull: University of Hull School of Adult and Continuing Education, 1987. 211 transcripts.

Lincoln

JOHNSTON, J.A., ed. *Probate inventories of Lincoln citizens, 1661-1714.* L.R.S. **80**, 1991.

MADDISON, A.R. 'Abstracts of wills proved in the court of the Dean and Chapter of Lincoln and the Probate Court', *L.N.Q.* **11**, 1911, 180-90. Mostly inhabitants of the Cathedral Close.

Market Rasen

NEAVE, DAVID, ed. *Tudor Market Rasen: life and work in a sixteenth century market town illustrated by probate inventories.* Market Rasen: Market Rasen W.E.A.; Hull: University of Hull Dept of Adult Education, 1985. Includes transcript of 65 inventories.

Winteringham

NEAVE, DAVID, ed. *Winteringham, 1650-1760: life and work in a North Lincolnshire village, illustrated by probate inventories.* Winteringham: Workers Educational Association, 1984.

Individual wills

Many wills *etc.* relating to particular individuals or families have been separately published. These are listed here:

Ashmall

OLIVER, JAMES W. 'A local will', *Islonian* 2(4), 1989, 26. Will of John Ashmall of Epworth, 1731.

Ayscough

MADDISON, A.R. 'Will of Elizabeth Ayscough of City of Lincoln, dated 7 Dec. 1716', *L.N.Q.* 10, 1909, 201-2.

Barret

HEANLEY, ROBT. M. 'The will of Robert Barret of Wainfleet', *L.N.Q.* 3, 1893, 46-50. 1527.

Batlyng

HEANLEY, ROBT. M. 'Wainfleet records', *L.N.Q.* 4, 1896, 49-51. Will of John Batlyng, 1468.

Boothe

BARLEY, M.W. 'The Lincolnshire village and its buildings', *L.H.* 1, 1947-53, 252-72. Includes probate inventories of Thomas Boothe of Boston, 1571; John Swaine of Benington, 1636; Robert Chamberlin of Gedney, 1672 and William Clark of Wainfleet, 1709.

Brackenbury

'Unpublished wills', *M.G.H.* 2nd series 5, 1894, 133-4. Includes will of Carr Brackenbury of Spilsby, 1741.

Brakynburgh

'Will of Master John Brakynburgh, clerk', *L.N.Q.* 12, 1912, 63. 1487.

Brown

WATERS, R.E. CHESTER. 'Will of Matthias Brown of Horbling, 1662', *M.G.H.* N.S. 1, 1874, 441-3. Includes parish register extracts.

Bury

BURY, WILLIAM E. 'Bury of Grantham', *M.G.H.* 3rd series 3, 1900, 254-8; 4, 1902, 93-8. Wills, 16-18th c., also of Rutland, Northamptonshire and London.

Calcroft

'Will of John Calcroft, esq., 1772', *L.N.Q.* 23, 1936, 120-21.

Cecil

'Summaries of some wills and other genealogical data, illustrative of the connections between the families of Cecil and Harington in Lincolnshire in the XVI century, and subsequently in Rutlandshire ...', *M.G.H.* N.S. 3, 1880, 285-7.

Chamberlin

See Boothe

Cherrington

'Crowland inventory, 1730', *F.N.Q.* 4, 1898-1900, 193-4. Probate inventory of Stephen Cherrington.

Clark

See Boothe

Cracroft

See Palmer

Crispe

MADDISON, A.R. 'The following inventories are in the Muniment Room of the Dean and Chapter of Lincoln', *L.N.Q.* 7, 1904, 87. Probate inventories of John Crispe, 1645, Hugh Walter, 1680/1, and Walter Powell, 1690, all Lincoln Cathedral clergy.

Cromwell

FRIEDRICHS, RHODA L. 'The two last wills of Ralph, Lord Cromwell', *Nottingham medieval studies* 34, 1990, 93-112. 15th c., of Tattershall.

Dalison
'Will of Margaret Dalison, A.D. 1545', *L.N.Q.* 5, 1898, 119-21.

Deathe
MADDISON, A.R. 'A curious will', *L.N.Q.* 8, 1905, 246-7. Will of Roger Deathe, of Gosberton, 1608.

Dimock
H., J.C. 'An early Dymoke will', *L.N.Q.* 4, 1896, 11-13. Will of Leon Dymoke, 1512.
'Robert Dimock, mi^te^', *L.N.Q.* 4, 1896, 106-7. Will, 1543; of Scrivelsby.
'Will of Arthur Dymoke, A.D. 1558', *L.N.Q.* 5, 1898, 104-7. Of Toft Grange, Kirkby.

Ferne
POYNTON, E.M. 'The will of Sir John Ferne, knt.', *Genealogist* N.S. 21, 1905, 188-94. 1609.

Forman
MADDISON, A.R. 'Lincolnshire wills', *L.N.Q.* 7, 1904, 122-6. Will of Mary Forman of Upper Langton, 1637.

Freestone
MORIARTY, G. ANDREWS. 'Genealogical research in England: Freestone-Raithbeck-Thew', *New England historical and genealogical register* 72, 1918, 51-63 & 74, 1920, 140-46. See also 79, 1925, 170-75. Freestone, Raithbeck and Thew wills, 16th c., also includes extracts from Horncastle parish register, 1559-1639.

Haldin
'Will of John Haldin, 14 March 1503', *L.N.Q.* 22, 1934, 114-20. Of Burgh le Marsh.

Harington
See Cecil

Harrison
SIMPSON, JUSTIN. 'Harrison of Sedbergh and Stamford', *N.G.* 1, 1895, 165-6. Will of Reginald Harrison, 1594.

Holand
SIMPSON, JUSTIN. 'Will of John Holand of Crowland', *F.N.Q.* 2, 1892-4, 150-52.

Holles
WOOD, A.C. 'The family of Gervase Holles', *A.A.S.R.P.* 40, 1930, 257-70. Includes wills of Gervase Holles, 1625, Frescheville Holles, 1630, and John Kington, 1617.

Hutton
SIMPSON, JUSTIN. 'Will of John Hutton M.A., rector of Dunsby, Co.Lincoln', *F.N.Q.* 2, 1892-4, 227-8.

Irby
FOSTER, W.E. 'Wills of Irby family', *F.N.Q.* 5, 1901-3, 8-12 & 40-43. Of Norfolk and Lincolnshire, 16-17th c.
FOSTER, W.E. *Abstracts of some wills of the Irby and Tashe families.* Peterborough: Geo. C. Carter, 1901. Reprinted from *F.N.Q.* 15-17th c.

Kay
MADDISON, A.R. 'Will of Joan Kay, widow, of Stixwold', *L.N.Q.* 3, 1905, 73-5. 1525.

Kent
KENT, P. RAMSEY. 'Kent family wills', *L.N.Q.* 3, 1893, 205-7. See also 247-9. 17th c. abstracts.

Kington
See Holles

Lake
WHITMORE, WILLIAM H. 'Lake family', *New England historical and genealogical register* 18, 1864, 131-2. Will of Sir Edward Lake, Bt., 1665.

Meres
DEACON, EDWARD. 'The Meres family', *L.N.Q.* 4, 1896, 191-2. Will of Thomas Meres, of Kirton, 1484.

Monson
MADDISON, A.R. 'Monson wills', *L.N.Q.* 9, 1907, 29-32. Will of Jane Monson, 1670.

Newcomen
FLETCHER, W.G.D. 'Family of Newcomen of Co.Lincoln', *Genealogist* 7, 1883, 229-31. Wills and inquisitions post mortem, 16-18th c.

Ornsby

G., S.G. 'The will of Anne Ornsby', *L.N.Q.* **19**, 1928, 108-9. Of South Kelsey, 1711.

Palmer

MADDISON, A.R. 'Will of Jane Palmer of Boston, widow of Laurence Palmer, merchant, and previously widow of John Cracroft of Ingoldmells', *L.N.Q.* **8**, 1905, 3-5. 1557/8.

Powell

See Crispe

Raithbeck

See Freestone

Ravenser

PRETYMAN, RICHARD. 'Testamentary documents preserved in the Chapter Room, in Lincoln Minster: the will and inventories of the effects of Richard de Ravenser, Archdeacon of Lincoln, 1386', in *Memoirs illustrative of the history and antiquities of the County and City of Lincoln ...* Archaeological Institute of Great Britain and Ireland, 1850, 311-27.

Robinson

WILLIAMS, I.L. 'John Robinson: a postscript', *L.F.H.S.M.* 4(1), 1993, 11-12. Probate inventory, 1674.

Sanders

'Sanders wills', *F.N.Q.* **5**, 1901-3, 192-3. 18th c.

Saunderson

MADDISON, A.R. 'Saunderson family', *L.N.Q.* **6**, 1901, 86-9. Wills of Sir Nicholas Saunderson, 1629, and George Saunderson, 1636; includes brief pedigree, 16th c.

Skipwith

MADDISON, A.R. 'Abstract of the will of Dame Elizabeth Skipwith', *L.N.Q.* **8**, 1905, 38-41. 1697; includes pedigree, 17th c.

Smyth

A., F.S. 'Will of William Smyth, lately Bishop of Lincoln', *Cheshire sheaf* 3rd series **18**, 1923, 47.

Sturmy

MADDISON, A.R. 'Abstract of the will of Thomas Sturmy', *L.N.Q.* **9**, 1907, 154-6. 1710; includes pedigree, 17th c.

Suaby

WELBY, ALFRED. 'Will of John de Suaby, clerk, 1279', *L.N.Q.* **23**, 1936, 97-9. Of Swaby.

Swaine

See Boothe

Tache

FOSTER, W.E. 'Wills of Tache family', *F.N.Q.* **5**, 1901-3, 43-6. 15-16th c.

Tashe

See Irby

Tempest

TEMPEST, E.B. 'An old Lincolnshire will and its maker', *L.N.Q.* **3**, 1893, 52-5. Will of John Tempest, of Gosberton, 1522.

Thew

See Freestone

Thorald

MADDISON, A.R. 'An early Lincoln will, A.D. 1280', *L.N.Q.* **4**, 1896, 99-100. Will of Johannes Nepos Thoraldi ciuis Lincoln.

Todd

PEACOCK, EDWARD. 'Robert Todd, of Bicker: a Lincolnshire yeoman of the XVI century', *Reliquary* **12**, 1871-2, 148-51. Includes will and probate inventory, 1546.

Tyrwhit

MADDISON, A.R. 'Will of Faith Tyrwhit of Scrivelsby, widow', *L.N.Q.* **6**, 1901, 60-62. 1669.

Walter

See Crispe

Warwick

SIMPSON, JUSTIN. 'Richard Warwick, Alderman of Stamford', *F.N.Q.* **3**, 1895-7, 153-5. Will, 1684.

Wellyngore

WELBY, ALFRED E. 'Will of Richard Wellyngore of Denton, proved 1482', *L.N.Q.* **10**, 1909, 99-101.

Willerton

WILLERTON, JAMES. *Willerton wills and administrations recorded at the Principal Probate Registry, 1858-1982.* Willerton family history **8**. London: [ ], 1986. Abstracts.

WILLERTON, JAMES. *Willerton wills and administrations recorded in the Lincolnshire indexes.* Willerton family history **10**. Brough: [ ], 1982. Abstracts.

WILLERTON, JAMES. *Willerton wills & administrations proved & granted in the Prerogative Court of Canterbury.* Willerton family history **11**. London: [ ], 1988. Abstracts.

Wilson

'An almswoman's inventory', *F.N.Q.* **7**, 1907-9, 126-7. Probate inventory of Joan Wilson of Spalding, 1606.

Wotton

WELBY, ALFRED C.E. 'Will of Master Thomas Wotton, S.T.B., 1551', *L.N.Q.* **15**, 1919, 14-16.

Inquisitions Post Mortem

Inquisitions post mortem were taken on the deaths of 'tenants in chief' of the Crown, prior to 1646. They normally record the name of the heir, and list lands held. For Lincolnshire inquisitions, see:

MASSINGBERD, W.O. 'Early Lincolnshire inquisitions post mortem', *A.A.S.R.P.* **25**(1), 1899, 1-35.

BOYD, W., ed. 'Inquisitions P.M., Co.Lincoln temp. Henry VII', *L.N.Q.* **3**, 1893, 138-9, 186-9, 217-8; **4**, 1896, 8-11, 107-9.

BOYD, W. 'Lincolnshire inquisitions post mortem, temp. Henry VII', *A.A.S.R.P.* **23**(1), 1895, 1-80.

A few inquisitions relating to particular individuals or families have been separately published:

Dymoke

MASSINGBERD, W.O. 'Dymoke estates in Lincolnshire before 1650', *N.G.* **1**, 1895, 193-205. Inquisitions post mortem, with extracts from the royalist composition papers, 1640s.

M[ASSINGBERD], W.O. 'Dymokes of Friskney and Fulletby: inquisitions', *L.N.Q.* **4**, 1896, 210-13. Inquisitions post mortem, 16th c.

Eland

M., H. 'Eland family', *L.N.Q.* **6**, 1901, 175-9. Inquisition post mortem of Robert Eland, 1522.

Ferne

POYNTON, E.M. 'Sir John Ferne', *Genealogist* N.S. **12**, 1896, 251-3. Inquisition post mortem, 1609.

Gresham

'Family of Gresham: abstract of inquisitions post mortem', *M.G.H.* N.S. **3**, 1880, 85-7, 109-10, 146-8, 186-7 & 216-7. Also from various other counties, 16-17th c.

11. DIRECTORIES, MAPS AND DIALECT

A. Directories

The trade directories of the nineteenth and early twentieth centuries are the equivalent of the modern telephone book; they enable you to locate people in time and place. I have endeavoured to identify all those published in the nineteenth century and earlier which contain information of genealogical value. Selected directories of the early twentieth century are also included in the following list, which is arranged chronologically and by place. In general, directories which cover more than a few counties are not listed; these may be identified in the works listed in section 13 of the companion volume to the present work, *English genealogy: an introductory bibliography*, or in:

'List of directories covering East Midlands region up to 1900', *Bulletin of local history: East Midlands region* 3, 1968, 20-37. Covers Derbyshire, Leicestershire, Lincolnshire, Nottinghamshire and Rutland. Brief summary; no locations.

Pigot and Co's national commercial directory, comprising a directory and classification of the merchants, bankers, professional gentlemen, manufacturers and traders in ... Bedfordshire, Huntingdonshire, Cambridgeshire, Lincolnshire, Northamptonshire ... J. Pigot & Co., 1830. Reprinted as: *National commercial directory: Bedfordshire, Huntingdonshire, Cambridgeshire, Lincolnshire, Northamptonshire: Pigot and Co., 1830.* Kings Lynn: Michael Winton, 1992.

WHITE, WILLIAM & CO. *The history and directory of the towns and principal villages in the County of Lincoln, including the port of Kingston-upon-Hull and the adjacent towns and villages ...* ed. William Parson. Leeds: William White & Co., 1826.

Post Office directory of Lincolnshire, with Derbyshire, Leicestershire, Nottinghamshire and Rutlandshire. W. Kelly & Co., 1849-1937. Many issues. The Lincolnshire portion was sometimes published separately or combined with other counties. Title varies; sometimes *Kelly's directory ...*

Slater's (late Pigot & Co.) royal national commercial directory and topography of Yorkshire and Lincolnshire ... Manchester: Isaac Slater, 1849.

Hagar and Co's commercial directory of the market towns of Lincolnshire ... Nottingham: Stevensons for Hagar and Co., 1849.

Slaters (late Pigot & Co.) royal national and commercial directory of the counties of Bedfordshire, Cambridgeshire, Huntingdonshire, Lincolnshire, Norfolk, Northampton and Suffolk ... Manchester: Isaac Slater, 1850.

WHITE, WILLIAM. *History, gazetteer and directory of Lincolnshire ...* 2nd ed. Sheffield: W. White, 1852. Reprinted as *White's 1856 Lincolnshire.* Newton Abbot: David & Charles, 1969. Also reprinted on microfiche, Melbourne: English Census Directories Project, 1991. (6 fiche.)

Slater's late Pigot & Co's royal national commercial directory, containing every city, town and principal village in the County of Lincolnshire ... Manchester: Isaac Slater, 1857.

Morris & Co's commercial directory & gazetteer of Lincolnshire. Nottingham: Morris & Co., 1863-66. 2 issues.

Mercer and Crocker's general, topographical and historical directory and gazetteer for Lincolnshire, with Hull, &c. ... Hull: Mercer and Crocker, 1870.

Lincolnshire 1872 history and directory/William White Limited: a part reproduction comprising Lincoln and eight Wapentakes. With introduction by Michael Winton. Kings Lynn: Hindsight Publications, 1988. Originally published 1872.

Bennett's business directory for Lincolnshire. Birmingham: Bennett & Co., 1899-1912. Almost annual.

Lincoln, Grimsby and district trades directory. Edinburgh: Town and County Directories, 1915/16-1928/9. 2 issues.

Lincolnshire directory, 1928. Walsall: Aubrey & Co., 1928.

Gainsborough

Cook's Gainsborough & Retford directory, with the surrounding villages ... Boston: W.J. Cook & Co., 1893.

Grantham

Grantham and District directory, containing street, officials, private residents, alphabetical and classified trades directories. Shrewsbury: Wells & Manton, 1887.

Grantham directory and the surrounding villages ... Boston: W.J. Cook & Co., 1892-1901. 5 issues; title varies.

The Grantham red book and street directory, with almanack and diary. Grantham: Clarke and Marshall, 1902.

Needham Bros. illustrated almanac and directory, diary and local advertiser. Grantham: Needham Bros, 1907-13. The 1907 edition states '28th year of publication', but earlier issues have not been seen. Continued by *Harrison's illustrated almanack for Grantham* ... Grantham: W.C. Harrison, 1915-45. Annual.

Grimsby

Tesseyman's directory and handbook to the Port of Grimsby ... Grimsby: William Tesseyman, 1852.

The Post Office directory of Grimsby & Cleethorpes ... Great Grimsby: Albert Gait, 1880.

A directory of Great Grimsby & Cleethorpes ... Great Grimsby: Albert Gait, 1871.

White's directory of Grimsby and neighbourhood. 8th ed. Sheffield: Wm. White, 1895. No other editions located.

Humberside

WHITE, WM. *Directory, guide and annals of Kingston-upon-Hull, Scarborough, Bridlington, Flambro', Filey, Hornsea, and the towns and ports connected with the Rivers Humber, Ouse and Trent, including Grimsby, Louth, Barton, Brigg, Gainsborough, Goole, Howden, Selby, Thorne, Snaith, Market-Weighton, Pocklington, Beverley, Caves, Driffield, Hedon, Patrington, and the adjacent towns and villages* ... Sheffield: William White, 1831.

General directory and topography of Kingston-upon-Hull and the City of York, with Beverley, Bridlington, Driffield, Scarborough, Whitby, Malton, Pocklington, Market Weighton, Goole, Howden, Selby, Snaith, Thorne, Doncaster, Great Grimsby, Barton, Brigg, Gainsborough, Louth, Market

Rasen, Crowle, Epworth, Kirton-in-Lindsey, &c., &c. ... Sheffield: Francis White & Co., 1851.

Lincoln

The Lincoln commercial directory and private residence guide. Lincoln: Victor and Baker, 1843.

The City of Lincoln directory. Lincoln: Charles Akrill, 1857-1932. Publisher varies; issued every 5-10 years.

City of Lincoln and District (embracing the surrounding villages within ten miles radius) directory ... Lincoln: Clifford Thomas, for W.J. Cook & Co., 1895.

B. Gazetteers, Place-Names and Maps

Gazetteers and maps are essential tools for the genealogist. The county maps of parish boundaries published by the Institute of Heraldic and Genealogical Studies are particularly useful. For a gazetteer specifically intended for the family historian see:

BRANSON, SAM. *A gazetteer of historic Lincolnshire for family and local historians.* Grantham: L.F.H.S., 1993.

See also:

NOBLE, JOSEPH. *The gazetteer of Lincolnshire, historical, topographical and antiquarian* ... Hull: Joseph Noble, 1833. Includes brief historical and geographical notes on each parish.

List of localities: towns, parishes, hamlets, etc. 6th ed. Lincoln: Lincolnshire County Council, 1980. Gazetteer.

CAMERON, KENNETH. *The place names of Lincolnshire.* English Place-Name Society **54/5-6 & 58.** 1985- v.1. Lincoln. v.2. Yarborough Wapentake. v.3. Walshcroft Wapentake. To be continued.

EMINSON, THOMAS BENJAMIN FRANKLIN. *The place and river names of the West Riding of Lindsey, Lincolnshire.* Lincoln: J.W. Ruddock & Sons, 1934.

For maps see:

The old series Ordnance Survey maps of England and Wales ... *volume V: Lincolnshire, Rutland and East Anglia.* Lympne Castle: Harry Margary, 1987.

BENNETT, STEWART, & BENNETT, NICHOLAS, eds. *An historical atlas of Lincolnshire.* Hull: University of Hull Press, 1993. General history of the county using maps.

GOSHAWK, PETER. 'Old Lincolnshire maps',
L.H. 1(3), 1948, 78-91.

C. *Dialect*

You may well come across dialect words in old
documents which you do not understand. A
number of dictionaries are available to help
you with these:

BROGDEN, J. ELLETT. *Provincial words and
expressions current in Lincoln.* Robert
Hardwicke, 1866.

COLE, R.E.G. *A glossary of words used in
South-West Lincolnshire (Wapentake of
Graffoe).* Trübner & Co., for the English
Dialect Society, 1886.

GOOD, JABEZ. *A glossary or collection of
words, phrases, place names, superstitions,
&c., current in East Lincolnshire.* 3rd ed.
Skegness: Skegness Publicity Service, 1973.
Originally published Long Sutton: H.
Pulford, 1911.

PEACOCK, EDWARD. *A glossary of words used
in the Wapentakes of Manley and
Corringham, Lincolnshire.* Series C, 6.
Trübner & Co., for the English Dialect
Society, 1877.

12. OFFICIAL LISTS OF NAMES

The bureaucratic methods of government
frequently involve the compilation of lists of
names. This is not a modern phenomenon; the
earliest such surviving list is Domesday book,
compiled in 1086. There are a number of
editions of both this and its twelfth century
successor, the Lindsey survey, both of which
identify manorial lords:

MORGAN, PHILIP, & THORN, CAROLINE, eds.
Domesday book, 31: Lincolnshire. 2 vols.
Chichester: Phillimore & Co., 1986.

FOSTER, C.W., & LONGLEY, THOMAS, eds. *The
Lincolnshire Domesday and the Lindsey
survey.* L.R.S. 19. 1924. The Lindsey survey
is dated 1115-18.

'The Lindsey survey (1115-1118)', in ROUND, J.H.
*Feudal England: historical studies on the
XIth and XIIth centuries.* Swan Sonneschein
& Co., 1895, 181-95.

GREENSTREET, JAMES, ed. *The Lincolnshire
survey, temp. Henry I.* Wyman & Sons, 1884.

WATERS, ROBERT EDMOND CHESTER. *A roll of
the owners of land in the parts of Lindsey
in Lincolnshire in the reign of Hen I.*
Williamson, 1883. Reprinted from *A.A.S.R.P.*
16(2), 1882, 116-230.

Tax Lists

From the medieval period until the
seventeenth century, the subsidy provided one
of the major sources of government revenue.
Each time it was levied, returns of those
paying were compiled. Surviving returns for
Lincolnshire are now in the Public Record
Office, and are listed in:

'A calendar of Exchequer lay subsidies in the
Public Record Office', *L.N.Q.* 9, 1907, 171-9,
210-19 & 235-42; 10, 1909, 11-17 & 38-45. See
also 9, 1907, 205-9.

Many Lincolnshire tax lists have been
published. They are listed here in
chronological order:

WELBY, A.C.E. 'Lincolnshire knightly surnames
temp. Henry II', *L.N.Q.* 3, 1893, 16-20. Names
from an Aid of Henry II.

CAZEL, FRED A., & CAZEL, ANNARIE P., eds.
*Rolls of the fifteenth of the 9th year of the
reign of Henry III for Cambridgeshire,
Lincolnshire and Wiltshire ...* Publications of

the Pipe Roll Society **83**. N.S. **45**. 1983 (for 1976-7). The Lincolnshire portion is concerned with Aswardhurn Wapentake only.

MASSINGBERD, W.O. 'Roll of the Wapentake of Yarborough', *L.N.Q.* **6**, 1901, 215-8 & 244-55; **7**, 1904, 16-30 & 35. Lists lords; perhaps the original return for the hundred rolls of Edward I.

McHARDY, A.K., ed. *Clerical poll-taxes of the Diocese of Lincoln, 1377-1381.* L.R.S. **81**. 1992.

PLATTS, GRAHAM. 'Butterwick and the poll taxes of 1377 and 1380', *L.H.A.* **24**, 1989, 5-16. Includes transcripts and detailed commentary.

WELBY, ALFRED C.E. 'Knights holding land in Lincolnshire, 1428, 1431', *L.N.Q.* **12**, 1912, 11-14. From *Feudal aids.*

WELBY, ALFRED C.E. 'Subsidy roll, 1436', *L.N.Q.* **12**, 1912, 54-9, 76-81.

SALTER, H. *A subsidy collected in the Diocese of Lincoln in 1526.* Oxford Historical Society **63**. 1909. Clerical subsidy, listing clergy of the Diocese; Lincolnshire occupies 1-94. For further clerical subsidies, see Foster's *State of the church ...* below, section 13B.

SIMPSON, JUSTIN. 'Lincolnshire contributors to the royal loan to Charles I, 1625', *Reliquary* **25**, 1884-5, 14-16.

B[OYD], W., ed. 'Exchequer subsidies (lay) County of Lincoln: Eliz to Car II ... Hearth money, ... Parts of Kesteven', *L.N.Q.* **4**, 1896, 71-4.

'Proceedings on account of ye rebellion in 1745', *L.N.Q.* **12**, 1912, 238-41. Lists contributors to a 'voluntary' subscription in aid of the crown.

GRIGG, D.B. 'The land tax returns', *Agricultural history review* **11**, 1963, 82-94. Discussion of the returns for the Parts of Kesteven and Holland as an historical source.

MILLS, DENNIS. 'Early land tax assessments explored (1): Rutland, Cambridgeshire and Lincolnshire', in TURNER, M., & MILLS, D., eds. *Land and property: the English land tax, 1692-1832.* New York: St.Martins Press, 1986, 189-203. General discussion of assessments as a source.

CARTWRIGHT, J.J. 'List of persons in Lincolnshire who paid the tax on male servants in 1780', *L.N.Q.* **4**, 1896, 200-207.

Loyalty Oaths

From time to time, governments demand oaths of loyalty from their subjects. The so-called 'protestation' oath was ordered by Parliament in 1641/2, at the outbreak of the Civil War; all adult males were required to sign the oath, and most of their signatures (or marks) are still preserved in the House of Lords Record Office. The returns for Lincolnshire are in print; see:

WEBSTER, W.F., [ed.] *Protestation returns, 1641/2: Lincolnshire.* Nottingham: Technical Print Services, 1984.

For a brief discussion of the Lincolnshire returns, see also:

WEST, F. 'The Protestation returns of 1642', *Bulletin of local history: East Midlands Region* **6**, 1971, 50-54.

Electoral records

Poll books and electoral registers are not listed here; to identify them consult the works listed in my *English genealogy: an introductory bibliography* section 12D. Two related works are:

ROGERS, ALAN. 'Parliamentary elections in Grimsby in the fifteenth century', *Bulletin of the Institute of Historical Research* **42**, 1969, 212-20. Gives names of electors, from the Corporation records.

ROGERS, ALAN. 'Parliamentary electors in Lincolnshire in the fifteenth century', *L.H.A.* **3**, 1968, 41-79; **4**, 1969, 33-53; **5**, 1970, 47-58; **6**, 1971, 67-81. Biographical dictionary of Parliamentary electors.

The Census

By far the most useful lists of names are those deriving from the official censuses. A brief guide to these, listing studies based on them, is provided by:

MILLS, DENNIS R. 'A Lincolnshire guide to the nineteenth-century censuses', *L.H.A.* **22**, 1987, 25-9.

Two interesting studies based on the census are:

MILLS, DENNIS, & MILLS, JOAN. 'Rural mobility in the Victorian census: experience with a micro-computer program', *Local historian* **18**, 1988, 69-75. Methodological study using some Lincolnshire and Buckinghamshire villages for a case study.

STEEL, DAVID. 'One hundred years on: the use of a private census to compare with the mid-nineteenth century enumerators' returns', *Local historian* 12(2), 1976, 93-101. Study of Corby Glen.

A number of private censuses *etc.*, were taken in the late eighteenth/early nineteenth centuries. See:

'Local census listings: Swinderby (1)', *L.F.H.S.M.* 4(1), 1993, 8-10. 'Census' of 1771.

'Holbeach householders, 1801', *F.N.Q.* 2, 1892-4, 342-3. List names from a rare survival of the 1801 returns.

PADDISON, PETER. 'The 1836 'census' of Marsh Chapel', *L.F.H.S.M.* 3(3), 1992, 104-5 & 3(4), 1992, 160. Private census.

The census enumerators' returns for Skegness are printed in:

The parish of Skegness: census enumerators returns for 1841, 1861, 1871, with surname index. Skegness: South-East Lindsey Teachers Centre, [1981].

Most Lincolnshire censuses have been comprehensively indexed. In order to use these indexes, you may need to check first:

RATCLIFFE, RICHARD E.B., & ANDREW, M.B. *Registration districts of Lincolnshire in the nineteenth century.* [ ]: Lincolnshire Family History Society, 1990.

The following published indexes are available:

1851
RATCLIFFE, R.E.B., ed. *Alphabetical index of surnames in the 1851 census of Lincolnshire.* 12 pts. [Lincoln]: S.L.H.A. Family History Sub-Committee, 1983-6. Reprinted by L.F.H.S. as *1851 census of Lincolnshire: index of surnames.*

1871
RATCLIFFE, RICHARD E.B. *1871 census of Lincolnshire: index of surnames.* 14 vols. [Lincoln]: S.L.H.A. Family History Committee/L.F.H.S., 1989-92.

1881
RATCLIFFE, RICHARD E.B., ed. *1881 census of Lincolnshire: surname index.* 14 vols. Gainsborough: Society for Lincolnshire History and Archaeology. Family History Committee, 1986-8.

RATCLIFFE, RICHARD. 'Beyond the 1881 census', *S.L.H.A.F.H.S.N.* 6(1), 1987, 24-6. Lists staff and patients in the County Hospital, Lincoln, from the 1881 census.

1891
EMPTAGE, EILEEN & EMPTAGE, ERIC. *1891 census of Lincolnshire: index of surnames.* 14 vols. Lincoln: L.F.H.S., 1992-3.

Landowners
A different type of census was taken in 1873. Everyone who owned an acre or more of land was listed, and the returns were published in the Parliamentary papers. See:

'Lincoln' in *Return of owners of land, 1873: vol.1.* House of Commons Parliamentary paper, 1874, LXXII, pt.1. 723-830.

13. ECCLESIASTICAL RECORDS

A. General

Church records are of the greatest importance to genealogists. This reflects the fact that ecclesiastical involvement in the life of society was formerly much wider than it is today. Some ecclesiastical records, i.e. parish registers, probate records, estate records, and churchwardens' accounts, are dealt with in other sections of this book. Here, the focus is on those records which are more directly concerned with ecclesiastical matters.

There are many works on different aspects of diocesan history. For a general introduction, see:

VENABLES, EDMUND, & PERRY, GEORGE G. *Lincoln*. Diocesan histories. S.P.C.K., 1897.
For the bishops of Lincoln, see:
PERRY, G.G., & VENABLES, J.H. *Biographical notices of the Bishops of Lincoln from Remigius to Wordsworth*. Lincoln: G. Gale, 1900. Reprinted 1972.

The following list of works on diocesan history which may be of interest to genealogists is arranged in rough chronological order.

SMITH, DAVID M., ed. *English episcopal acta, I: Lincoln, 1067-1185*. Oxford University Press for the British Academy, 1980.
WILLIAMSON, DOROTHY M. '*Sede vacante* records of the Diocese of Lincoln', *Society of Local Archivists bulletin* 12, 1953, 13-20.
SHRAWLEY, J.H., ed. *The book of John de Schalby, canon of Lincoln (1299-1333) concerning the Bishops of Lincoln and their acts*. Lincoln Minster pamphlets 2. Lincoln: Friends of Lincoln Cathedral, 1949.
MAJOR, KATHLEEN. 'The finances of the Dean and Chapter of Lincoln from the twelfth to the fourteenth century: a preliminary survey', *Journal of ecclesiastical history* 5, 1954, 149-67. Includes discussion of sources which may be of genealogical value.
MORRIS, COLIN. 'The commissary of the bishop of the Diocese of Lincoln', *Journal of ecclesiastical history* 10, 1959, 50-65. Medieval; includes brief discussion of the court's probate powers.

MORRIS, COLIN. 'A consistory court in the middle ages', *Journal of ecclesiastical history* 14, 1963, 150-59. General discussion.
GRAVES, COBURN V. 'English Cistercian nuns in Lincolnshire', *Speculum* 54, 1979, 492-9. Brief discussion.
WORDSWORTH, CHR. 'Lincolnshire chantries', *N.G.* 1, 1895, 152-5. Brief notes on a survey.
SMITH, DAVID M. 'Hugh's administration of the Diocese of Lincoln', in MAYR-HARTING, HENRY, ed. *St.Hugh of Lincoln: lectures delivered at Oxford and Lincoln to celebrate the eighth centenary of St.Hugh's consecration as Bishop of Lincoln*. Oxford: Clarendon Press, 1987, 19-47. 12th c.
DYSON, A.G. 'The monastic patronage of Bishop Alexander of Lincoln', *Journal of ecclesiastical history* 26, 1975, 1-24. General discussion, 12th c.
BURGER, MICHAEL. '*Officiales* and the *familiae* of the bishops of Lincoln, 1258-1299', *Journal of medieval history* 16(1), 1990, 39-53. General discussion; includes useful references.
HILL, ROSALIND. 'Bishop Sutton and his archives: a study in the keeping of records in the thirteenth century', *Journal of ecclesiastical history* 2(1), 1951, 43-53. General study.
HILL, ROSALIND. 'Bishop Sutton and the institution of heads of religious houses in the Diocese of Lincoln', *English historical review* 58, 1943, 201-9. Includes a list of heads instituted, 1280-99.
THOMPSON, A. HAMILTON. 'Pluralism in the medieval church, with notes on pluralists in the Diocese of Lincoln, 1366', *A.A.S.R.P.* 33(1), 1915, 35-73; 34(1), 1917, 1-26; 35(1), 1918, 87-108; 35(2), 1920, 199-242; 36(1), 1921, 1-41.
McHARDY, A.K. 'Notes on a neglected source: a register of royal writs in the Lincoln Diocesan archives', *L.H.A.* 16, 1981, 25-7. 14th c., discussion only.
BOWKER, MARGARET. 'Non-residence in the Lincoln Diocese in the early sixteenth century', *Journal of ecclesiastical history* 15, 1964, 40-50. General discussion.
THOMPSON, A.H. 'Visitations of religious houses by William Alnwick, Bishop of Lincoln, 1436-49', *Proceedings of the Society of Antiquaries* 2nd series 26, 1914, 89-103.

BOWKER, MARGARET. *The secular clergy in the Diocese of Lincoln, 1495-1520.* Cambridge: Cambridge University Press, 1968. Includes various lists of clergy, and useful bibliography.

BOWKER, MARGARET. *The Henrician Reformation: the Diocese of Lincoln under John Longland, 1521-1547.* Cambridge: Cambridge University Press, 1981.

BOWKER, MARGARET. 'The Henrician Reformation and the parish clergy', *Bulletin of the Institute of Historical Research* **50**, 1977, 30-47. General discussion of the impact of the Reformation on the clergy of the Diocese of Lincoln.

KNIGHT, FRANCES. 'Ministering to the ministers: the discipline of recalcitrant clergy in the Diocese of Lincoln, 1830-1845', in SHEILS, WILLIAM J., & WOOD, DIANA, eds. *The ministry: clerical and lay.* Studies in church history **26**. Oxford: Blackwell, 1989, 357-66.

BONNEY, H.K. *Bonney's church notes, being notes on the churches in the Archdeaconry of Lincoln, 1845-1848.* ed. N.S. Harding. Lincoln: Keyworth & Sons, 1937. General guide, with little of direct genealogical interest.

The study of church bells and their inscriptions can yield much useful information; inscriptions provide many names of clergy, churchwardens, bellfounders, donors, *etc.* The standard work for Lincolnshire is:

NORTH, THOMAS. *Church bells of the County and City of Lincoln: their founders, inscriptions, traditions and peculiar uses, with a brief history of church bells in Lincolnshire.* Leicester: Samuel Clarke, 1882.

See also:

KETTERINGHAM, JOHN R. 'Dead ringers (or campanological sources)', *Family tree magazine* **10**(5), 1994, 45. Based on Lincolnshire sources.

KETTERINGHAM, JOHN R. 'Lincolnshire church bell inscriptions and the effect of change', *L.P.P.* **1**, 1990, 14-18.

B. *Diocesan Archives and Original Sources*

The extensive archives of the Diocese of Lincoln are listed in:

MAJOR, KATHLEEN. *A handlist of the records of the Bishop of Lincoln and of the Archdeacons of Lincoln and Stow.* Oxford University Press, 1953.

See also:

MADDISON, A.R. 'The transcripts in the Bishop of Lincoln's registry', *A.A.S.R.P.* **16**(2), 1882, 159-66. General description of the Diocesan archives.

MAJOR, KATHLEEN. 'Lincoln Diocesan records as sources for the genealogist', *Genealogists' magazine* **9**(5), 1941, 158-71.

MAJOR, KATHLEEN. 'The Lincoln Diocesan records', *Transactions of the Royal Historical Society* **22**, 1940, 39-66.

MAJOR, KATHLEEN. 'Parish history from Diocesan records. 1. The clergy. 2. The laity', *Lincolnshire magazine* **3**, 1936-8, 331-4 & 374-9.

MAJOR, KATHLEEN. 'The Lincoln Diocesan Record Office', *L.A.A.S.R.P.* N.S. **3**, 1945, 12-17.

'The registry of the Bishop of Lincoln', in HISTORICAL MANUSCRIPTS COMMISSION. *Twelfth report, appendix, part IX: the manuscripts of the Duke of Beaufort, K.G., the Earl of Donoughmore, and others.* C.6338-I. H.M.S.O., 1891, 573-9.

BENNETT, J.A. 'The manuscripts of the Dean and Chapter of Lincoln', in HISTORICAL MANUSCRIPTS COMMISSION. *Twelfth report, appendix, part IX: the manuscripts of the Duke of Beaufort, K.G., the Earl of Donoughmore, and others.* C.6338-I. H.M.S.O., 1891, 553-72.

WILLIAMSON, DOROTHY M. *The muniments of the Dean and Chapter of Lincoln.* Lincoln Minster pamphlets **8**. Lincoln: Friends of Lincoln Cathedral, 1956. Survey of their history, rather than a list.

WICKENDEN, PREB. 'Contents of the muniments room of Lincoln Cathedral', *Archaeological journal* **28**, 1881, 309-15.

VARLEY, JOAN. 'Episcopal records with particular reference to the Diocese of Lincoln and Archdeaconry of Leicester', *Leicestershire Archaeological and Historical Society transactions* **46**, 1972, 45-64. Includes a list of 'printed sources and related books'.

Many editions of original sources from the diocesan archives have been published, and are listed here in rough chronological order:

SMITH, DAVID M., ed. *English episcopal acta, IV: Lincoln, 1186-1206.* Oxford University Press for the British Academy, 1986.

HOLTZMANN, WALTHER, ed. *Papal decretals relating to the Diocese of Lincoln in the twelfth century.* L.R.S. **47**. 1954.

PHILLIMORE, W.P.W., & DAVIS, F.N., eds. *Rotuli Hugonis de Welles, episcopi Lincolniensis, MCCIX-MCCXXXV.* Canterbury and York Society **1, 3** & **4**. 1907-9. Also issued as L.R.S. **3, 6** & **9**. 1912-14.

SMITH, DAVID. 'The rolls of Hugh of Wells, Bishop of Lincoln, 1209-35', *Bulletin of the Institute of Historical Research* **45**(112), 1972, 155-95. General discussion.

DIMOCK, JAMES F., ed. *Giraldi Cambrensis opera, vol.7.* Rolls series **21**. Longman & Co., *et al*, 1877. The appendix includes a 12th c. obituary of Lincoln Cathedral, John de Schalby's *Lives of the Bishops of Lincoln,* a list of *Indulgencies ... to contributors to Lincoln Cathedral* and the will of Hugh de Wells, Bishop of Lincoln, 1227.

DAVIS, F.N., ed. *Rotuli Roberti Grosseteste, episcopi Lincolniensis, A.D. MCCXXXV-MCCLIII.* Canterbury and York Society **10**. 1913. Also issued as L.R.S. **11**. 1914.

DAVIS, F.N., ed. *Rotuli Ricardi Gravesend, diocesis Lincolniensis.* Canterbury and York Society **31**. 1925. Also published as L.R.S. **20**. 1925. 1258-79.

HILL, ROSALIND M.T., ed. *The rolls and registers of Bishop Oliver Sutton, 1280-1299.* L.R.S. **39, 43, 48, 52, 60, 64, 69,** & **76**. 1948-86. v.39. Institution to beneficiaries and confirmations of heads of religious houses in the Archdeaconry of Lincoln. v.43. Ditto in the Archdeaconry of Northampton. v.48, 52, 60 & 64. Memoranda. v.69. Ordinations, May 19, 1290-September 19, 1299. v.76. Institutions, collations and sequestrations; all archdeaconries except Lincoln and Northampton.

ARCHER, MARGARET, ed. *The register of Bishop Philip Repingdon, 1405-1419.* L.R.S. **57-8** & **74**. 1963-82. v.1. Memoranda, 1405-1411. v.2. Memoranda, 1411-1414. v.3. Memoranda, 1414-1419.

BENNETT, N.H., ed. *The register of Richard Fleming, Bishop of Lincoln, 1420-31.* Canterbury and York Society **73**. 1984. v.1. only.

THOMPSON, A. HAMILTON, ed. *Visitations of religious houses in the Diocese of Lincoln.* 3 vols. Canterbury and York Society **17, 24** &

33. 1915-27. Also issued as L.R.S. **7, 14** & **21**. 1914-23. v.1. Injunctions and other documents from the registers of Richard Flemyng and William Gray, bishops of Lincoln, A.D. 1420-1436. v.2-3. Records of visitations held by William Alnwick, Bishop of Lincoln, A.D. 1436-1449.

CLARK, ANDREW, ed. *Lincoln Diocese documents, 1450-1544.* Early English Text Society, Original series **149**. 1914. Includes 37 wills, 8 leases, and much else.

BOWKER, MARGARET, ed. *An episcopal court book for the Diocese of Lincoln, 1514-1520.* L.R.S. **61**. 1967.

THOMPSON, A. HAMILTON, ed. *Visitation in the Diocese of Lincoln, 1517-1531.* L.R.S. **33, 35** & **37**. 1940-47. v.1. Visitations of rural deaneries by William Atwater, Bishop of Lincoln, and his commissaries, 1517-1520. v.2. Visitations of rural deaneries by John Longland, Bishop of Lincoln, and of religious houses by Bishops Atwater and Longland, and by his and their commissaries, 1517-1531. v.3. Visitations of religious houses ... (concluded)

HODGETT, G.A.J., ed. *The state of the ex-religious and former chantry priests in the Diocese of Lincoln, 1547-1574, from returns in the Exchequer.* L.R.S. **53**. 1959.

FOSTER, C.W. 'Certificate or return of all fees, annuities, corrodies, or pensions, payable to religious persons, 1555-6', *A.A.S.R.P.* **37**(2), 1925, 276-94.

FOSTER, C.W., ed. *Lincoln episcopal records in the time of Thomas Cooper, S.T.P., Bishop of Lincoln, A.D. 1571 to A.D. 1584.* L.R.S. **2**. 1912. Also published as Canterbury & York Society **11**. 1913. From various sources; includes ordinations, admissions to beneficies, grants of advowsons, presentations, lists of clergy, and Bishop Cooper's *Register, etc.*

FOSTER, C.W., ed. *The state of the church in the reigns of Elizabeth and James I, as illustrated by documents relating to the Diocese of Lincoln, vol.1.* L.R.S. **23**, 1926. No more published. Clerical subsidies, 1571-83, *libri cleri,* 1576-1607, *etc.* For further clerical subsidies see section 12 above.

HILL, J.W.F. 'The Royalist clergy of Lincolnshire', *L.A.A.S.R.P.* N.S. **2**, 1940, 34-127. Deposition taken before the Committee for Scandalous Ministers, 1640s; many names.

HOLTZMANN, WALTHER, ed. *Papal decretals relating to the Diocese of Lincoln in the twelfth century.* L.R.S. **47**. 1954.

FOSTER, W.E. *The plundered ministers of Lincolnshire, being extracts from the minutes of the Committee of Plundered Ministers.* Guildford: Billing & Sons, 1900. Mid-17th c. Arranged by parish, with many names of clergy.

COLE, R.E.G., ed. *Speculum dioeceseos Lincolniensis sub episcopis Gul. Wake et Edm. Gibson A.D. 1705-1723. Pt.1: Archdeaconries of Lincoln and Stow.* L.R.S. **4.** 1913. Replies to bishop's queries, giving names of clergy, *etc.*

VARLEY, JOAN. 'An Archidiaconal visitation of Stow, 1752', *L.A.A.S.R.P.* N.S. **3,** 1945, 144-76. Names clergy and churchwardens.

STONEHOUSE, W.B. *A Stow visitation: being notes on the churches in the Archdeaconry of Stow, 1845 ... together with the returns of the rural deans for the years 1850, 1851, 1852.* Lincoln: Keyworth and Sons, 1940. Includes some names, but not much of direct genealogical interest.

AMBLER, R.A., ed. *Lincolnshire returns of the census of religious worship, 1851.* L.R.S. **72.** 1979. Includes names of clergymen, *etc.*

C. *Clergy Lists: General*

A variety of lists *etc.* of clergy in the Diocese of Lincoln have been compiled. These include (in rough chronological order):

LE NEVE, JOHN. *Fasti ecclesiae Anglicanae 1066-1300, III: Lincoln.* comp. Diana E. Greenway. University of London, Institute of Historical Research, 1977.

LE NEVE, JOHN. *Fasti ecclesiae Anglicanae 1300-1541, I: Lincoln Diocese,* comp. H.P.F. King. Athlone Press, 1962.

THOMPSON, A. HAMILTON. 'Lambeth institutions to benefices: being a calendar of institutions to benefices in the old Diocese of Lincoln during vacancies of the episcopal see and during the visitations of the Diocese by the Archbishops of Canterbury as metropolitans, with collations of benefices made by the Archbishops *jure devoluto,* from the archiepiscopal registers in the library of Lambeth Palace, 1279-1532', *A.A.S.R.P.* **40,** 1930, 33-110.

FOSTER, C.W. 'Institutions to benefices in the Diocese of Lincoln', *A.A.S.R.P.* **39,** 1929, 179-216. 13th c., also includes supplement to 17th c. admission as published in v.30 (see below).

GIBBONS, A. *Liber antiquus de ordinationibus vicariarum tempore Hugonis Wells, Lincolniensis Episcopi, 1209-1235.* Lincoln: James Williamson, 1888.

MAJOR, K. 'Fifteenth century presentation deeds in the Lincoln Diocesan Record Office', in HUNT, R.W., PANTIN, W.A., & SOUTHERN, R.W., eds. *Studies in medieval history presented to Frederick Maurice Powicke.* Oxford: Clarendon Press, 1948, 455-64. Study of a potentially useful source.

FOSTER, C.W. 'Institutions to benefices in the Diocese of Lincoln, 1540-1570. Calendar no.I', *A.A.S.R.P.* **24**(1), 1897, 1-32; **24**(2), 1898, 467-525. Includes index.

FOSTER, C.W. 'Institutions to benefices in the Diocese of Lincoln in the sixteenth century', *L.N.Q.* **5,** 1898, 129-44, 164-81, 191-209, 227-43; **6,** 1901, 3-19, 45-53, 78-85, 102-11 & 142-7. List, 1545-56. Continued in:

FOSTER, C.W. 'Institutions to benefices in the diocese of Lincoln, 1547-70. Calendar no.II', *A.A.S.R.P.* **25**(2), 1900, 459-544. Includes index.

FOSTER, C.W. 'Admissions to benefices in the Diocese of Lincoln, A.D. 1587-1660, as recorded in the bishops' certificates returned to the barons of the Exchequer', *A.A.S.R.P.* **30**(1), 1909, 47-118 & 379-90.

VENABLES, PRECENTOR. 'The primary visitation of the Diocese of Lincoln by Bishop Neile, A.D. 1614', *A.A.S.R.P.* **16**(1), 1881, 31-54. Includes list of ordinands, 1617-19, and names of 'lecturers', i.e. preachers, in the diocese.

BINNALL, PETER B.G. 'Bishop Sanderson's ordination book', *A.A.S.R.P.* N.S. **9,** 1961, 63-88. Lists clergy ordinations, 1660-62.

MAJOR, KATHLEEN. 'Resignation deeds of the Diocese of Lincoln', *Bulletin of the Institute of Historical Research* **19,** 1942-3, 57-65.

D. *Local Records, etc.*

Bardney Abbey
CROWDER, TOM. *Bardney Abbey: its history, charters, excavations, etc.* Horncastle: W.K. Morton & Sons, 1925. Includes notes on abbots, list of tombs, *etc.*

Candlesby
MASSINGBERD, W.O. 'Candlesby manor and advowson', *L.N.Q.* **6,** 1901, 71-7. Includes list of rectors, 1296-1834, with abstracts of various medieval inquisitions.

Carlton Hundred

DUDDING, R.C, 'The east Lindsey Carltons', *A.A.S.R.P.* **39**, 1929, 264-72 & **40**, 1930, 15-29. Carlton Hundred and the manors of Castle, Great and Little Carlton; includes lists of early incumbents and patrons.

Crowland

BOEUF, T.H. LE 'The rectors of Crowland since the dissolution of the monasteries', *F.N.Q.* **1**, 1889-91, 106-7. List.

Deeping St.James

SKENE, S.W. 'Deeping St.James vicarage', *F.N.Q.* **6**, 1904-6, 25-30. List of vicars.

Gedney

'Excommunications at Gedney', *F.N.Q.* **3**, 1895-7, 177-8. Recorded in the parish register, 17th c.

Graffoe Deanery

COLE, R.E.G. 'Notes on the ecclesiastical history of the Deanery of Graffoe to the close of the fourteenth century', *A.A.S.R.P.* **24**(2), 1898, 381-448. Includes list of institutions to benefices, 1209-1405.

COLE, R.E.G. 'Notes on the ecclesiastical history of the Deanery of Graffoe during the fifteenth and sixteenth centuries', *A.A.S.R.P.* **25**(1), 1899, 47-120; **25**(2), 1900, 253-309. Includes institutions to benefices, 1405-1705, *etc.*

COLE, R.E.G. 'Notes on the ecclesiastical history of Graffoe during the eighteenth and nineteenth centuries', *A.A.S.R.P.* **26**(1), 1901, 97-163. Includes institutions, 1705-1901.

Kettlethorpe

COLE, R.E.G. 'The manor and rectory of Kettlethorpe in the Parts of Lindsey in the County of Lincoln', *A.A.S.R.P.* **31**(1), 1911, 41-86. Includes list of rectors, pedigree of Swynford, 14-16th c., *etc.*

Lincoln Cathedral

COLE, R.E.G., ed. *Chapter acts of the Cathedral church of St.Mary of Lincoln ...* L.R.S. **12, 13 & 15**. 1915-20. v.1. 1520-36. v.2. 1536-47. v.3. 1547-59. Includes lists of dignitaries and prebendaries; and of deprivations; also clerical subsidy, 1526.

PRUETT, JOHN H. 'Career patterns among the clergy of Lincoln Cathedral, 1660-1750', *Church history* **44**, 1975, 204-16. General discussion.

MAJOR, KATHLEEN. 'The office of chapter clerk at Lincoln in the middle ages', in RUFFER, VERONICA, & TAYLOR, A.J., eds. *Medieval studies presented to Rose Graham.* Oxford: Oxford University Press, 1950, 163-88. Includes list of clerks, 13-16th c.

VENABLES, PRECENTOR. 'Bishop Antony Beeke's register of the Prebendaries of Lincoln, 1333, and 1343', *Archaeological journal* **42**, 1885, 469-75.

MADDISON, A.R. *A short account of the Vicars Choral, poor clerks, organists, and choristers of Lincoln Cathedral, from the 12th century to the accession of Edward VI.* Lincoln: [ ], 1878, Includes lists.

An historical account of the antiquities in the Cathedral church of St.Mary, Lincoln ... Lincoln: W. Wood, [1771]. Includes biographical notes on bishops, and notes on monumental inscriptions.

MADDISON, A.R. 'Lincoln Cathedral choir, A.D. 1558 to 1640', *A.A.S.R.P.* **18**(1), 1885, 110-22. Gives names of many vicars choral, with abstracts of the wills of Thomas Floure, 1555; William Freman, 1558, Robert Hurstcrofte, 1611, and George Huddleston, 1611.

MADDISON, A.R. 'Lincoln Cathedral choir, A.D. 1700-1750', *A.A.S.R.P.* **20**(2), 1890, 213-26. Includes names of vicars and choristers.

MADDISON, A.R. 'Lincoln Cathedral choir, A.D. 1750-1875', *A.A.S.R.P.* **21**(2), 1892, 208-26. Gives names of vicars choral; also includes a few monumental inscriptions.

ELVIN, LAURENCE. *The organists of Lincoln Cathedral, 1794-1986.* Lincoln: the author, 1986. Collection of biographies.

KETTERINGHAM, JOHN R. *Lincoln Cathedral: a history of the bells, bellringers and bellringing.* Lincoln: the author, 1987. Includes some names.

WORDSWORTH, PREB. 'The names of the companie of ringers of our Blessed Virgen Marie of Lincolne', *A.A.S.R.P.* **20**(2), 1890, 241-3. 1614-1725.

Louth

GOULDING, RD. W. *The vicars and the vicarage of Louth*. Louth: Goulding & Son, 1906.

Moulton

FOSTER, W.E. 'On the history of All Saints church, Moulton', *A.A.S.R.P.* **20**(2), 1890, 249-63. Includes list of vicars, *etc.*

FOSTER, W.E. 'Vicars of Moulton, Lincolnshire', *F.N.Q.* **5**, 1901-3, 325-7. List.

Norton Disney

'Institutions of Norton Disney, Co.Lincoln', *N.G.* **1**, 1895, 108-9.

Scremby

MASSINGBERD, W.O. 'Scremby institutions', *L.N.Q.* **6**, 1901, 179-88.

Sempringham

POYNTON, E.M. 'The nuns of Sempringham', *Genealogist* N.S. **18**, 1902, 110. List of nuns, 1366.

Sleaford

HOARE, DOUGLAS. 'Guide books to St.Dennys church, Sleaford', *S.L.H.A. newsletter* **59**, 1989, 23-5. Brief bibliographical guide.

Stamford

HOSKINS, J.P. 'The Dean of Stamford: a history of the office', *L.A.A.S.R.P.* N.S. **3**, 1945, 18-35. Includes list of deans.

PIPER, ALAN. 'St.Leonards Priory, Stamford', *Stamford historian* **5**, 1980, 5-25; **6**, 1982, 1-23. Includes list of priors.

Stow

SPURRELL, MARK. *Stow church restored, 1846-1866.* L.R.S. **75**. 1984. Letters concerning the restoration, giving many names.

D. *Nonconformity*

A number of works provide the names of early Lincolnshire dissenters:

LANGLEY, ARTHUR S. 'The Declaration of Indulgence, A.D. 1672: Lincolnshire licences', *L.N.Q.* **17**, 1923, 102-10. Lists persons granted licences to preach.

VARLEY, JOAN. 'Dissenters' certificates in the Lincoln Diocesan records', *L.H.* **4**, 1949, 167-77. Discussion of certificates for dissenters meeting houses, 18-19th c., with some names.

ROGERS, ALAN, & WATTS, MICHAEL. 'The Evans list and dissenting congregations in the East Midlands, 1715-29', *Bulletin of local history: East Midlands Region* **13**, 1978, 15-27. Lists dissenting ministers and their churches in Derbyshire, Leicestershire, Lincolnshire, Nottinghamshire, Rutland and Northamptonshire.

Huguenots

MINET, WILLIAM. 'The ministers of the church at Sandtoft', *Proceedings of the Huguenot Society of London* **13**, 1927, 408-10. Brief note.

Methodists

There are a number of useful works on the history of Lincolnshire Methodism. For general introductions, see:

LEARY, WILLIAM, & VICKERS, JOHN. *Methodist guide to Lincolnshire and East Anglia.* W.M.H.S. Publications, 1984.

LEARY, WILLIAM. *Lincolnshire Methodism.* Barracuda, 1988. General history.

See also:

AMBLER, R.W. *Ranters, revivalists and reformers: Primitive Methodism and rural society: South Lincolnshire, 1817-1875.* Hull: Hull University Press, 1989. Includes useful bibliography.

AMBLER, R.W. 'From Ranters to chapel builders: Primitive Methodism on the South Lincolnshire fenland, c.1820-1875', in SHEILS, W.J., & WOOD, DIANA, eds. *Voluntary religion.* Studies on church history **23**. Oxford: Blackwell, 1986, 319-31.

ROGERS, ALAN. 'When city speaks for county: the emergence of the town as a focus for religious activity in the nineteenth century', in BAKER, D., ed. *The church in town and countryside.* Studies in church history **16**. Oxford: Blackwell, 1979, 335-59. Study of Methodism in Lincolnshire.

LEARY, WILLIAM. 'Methodist people in the Isle of Axholme', *Islonian* **4**(3), 1992, 16-21; **4**(4), 1992, 23-6; **4**(5), 1993, 25-8; **4**(6), 1993, 12-16. Lists members in the Epworth Circuit, 1788-1911.

150 books on Lincolnshire Methodism are listed in: 'A bibliography', *Journal of the Lincolnshire Methodist History Society* 3(2), 1978, 37-41. Interesting articles on Methodism appear in: *The Epworth witness and journal of the Lincolnshire Methodist History Society*, 1963-76. 2 vols. Continued by: *Journal of the Lincolnshire Methodist History Society* 1977-

Two works list useful sources: LEACH, TERENCE. 'Methodist ancestors: some sources, part 2', *F.H.N.* 6, 1980, 6-7. Lists Lincolnshire obituary notices in various Methodist periodicals, 1778-1839.

'The beginnings of Methodism in Lincolnshire', *Journal of the Lincolnshire Methodist History Society* 4(1), 1988, 4-19. Includes extensive listing of early Methodist societies, from meeting house certificates; includes some names.

Boston

LEARY, WILLIAM. *Methodism in the town of Boston*. History of Boston series 6. Boston: Richard Kay Publications, 1972. Includes list of trustees, 19-20th c.

Horncastle

CLARKE, J.N., & ANDERSON, C.L. *Methodism in the Horncastle Circuit, 1786-1986.* Horncastle: the authors, 1986. Detailed general study; includes names of clergy and officers, *etc.*

Spalding

A faithful witness: a history of the Methodist Church, Broad Street, Spalding, 1888-1987. [Spalding: the Church, 1987.] Includes list of ministers, and a circuit plan, 1819, listing preachers.

Presbyterians

BOLAM, C. GORDON. *Three hundred years, 1662-1962: the story of the churches forming the North Midland Presbyterian and Unitarian Association.* Nottingham: Derry and Sons, [1962]. Includes lists of ministers at churches in Derbyshire, Leicestershire, Nottinghamshire and Lincolnshire.

Quakers

BRACE, HAROLD W., ed. *The first minute book of the Gainsborough monthly meeting of the Society of Friends, 1669-1719.* L.R.S. **38, 40** & **44.** 1948-51. Includes list of records.

KING-FANE, W.V.R. 'Some Lincolnshire Quakers in the 17th century', *Lincolnshire magazine* **2,** 1934-6, 321-5. Discussion of the evidence of minute books, 17th c.

DAVIES, SUSAN. *Quakerism in Lincolnshire: an informal history.* Lincoln: Yard Publication Services, 1989. General history; many names are noted.

Roman Catholics

'Some notes of Roman Catholics in Lincolnshire', *N.G.* **2,** 1896, 208; **3,** 1900, 102-4. Gives parishes, but few surnames, 1604-5 and 1780, from clergy returns.

GREEN, EVERARD. 'Some Lincolnshire martyrs', *L.N.Q.* **3,** 1893, 84-5. List of Roman Catholic martyrs, 16-17th c.

MIDDLEBROOK, MARTIN. *The Catholic church in Boston.* History of Boston series **15.** Boston: Richard Kay Publication, 1977. Includes list of priests, 1827-1977.

Jews

GERLIS, DAPHNE, & GERLIS, LEON. *The story of the Grimsby Jewish community.* Humberside Heritage publications **10.** Hull: Humberside Leisure Services, 1986. Includes list of clergy and synagogue officers.

14. RECORDS OF NATIONAL AND COUNTY ADMINISTRATION

Official lists of names, such as tax lists and census returns, have already been cited. There are, however, many other records of national and county government which provide useful information. A number of works list members of parliament:

WELBY, ALFRED. 'Knights of the shire, 1213-1327', *L.N.Q.* **21**, 1931, 123-8. List.

ROSKELL, J.S. 'The Parliamentary representation of Lincolnshire during the reigns of Richard II, Henry IV and Henry V', *Nottingham medieval studies* **3**, 1959, 53-77. General study.

ROGERS, ALAN. 'The Lincolnshire County Court in the fifteenth century', *L.H.A.* **1**, 1966, 64-78. Includes calendar of Parliamentary returns, listing sheriffs, M.P's, and witnesses of elections.

WELBY, ALFRED C.E. 'Lincolnshire members in the Long Parliament', *L.N.Q.* **11**, 1911, 53-7. Both county and borough members; includes biographical notes.

WELBY, ALFRED C.E. 'Lincolnshire members in the Cromwellian Parliaments', *L.N.Q.* **11**, 1911, 76-80. Includes brief biographical notes.

WELBY, ALFRED. 'Polls of Parliamentary county elections, 1705-1880', *L.N.Q.* **21**, 1931, 35-7. Lists M.P's.

For sheriffs, see:

FARRER, W. 'Sheriffs of Lincolnshire and Yorkshire, 1066-1130', *English historical review* **30**, 1915, 277-85.

KING-FANE, WILLIAM Y.R. *A list of the high sheriffs of Lincolnshire, 1154-1935.* Supplement to *L.N.Q.* **24**, 1936.

Chronological table of the high sheriffs of the County of Lincoln, and of the knights of the shire, citizens and burgesses in Parliament within the same from the earliest accounts to the present time. Joseph White, 1779.

WELBY, ALFRED. 'Sheriffs of Lincolnshire', *L.N.Q.* **22**, 1934, 99-102. List, 1833-1933.

Lord Lieutenants are listed in:

WELBY, ALFRED. 'Lords Lieutenants of Lincs from 1551', *L.N.Q.* **21**, 1931, 121-3.

Many transcripts, calendars, lists, indexes, *etc.,* of useful records have been published, and are listed here in rough chronological order:

'Assize rolls for the County of Lincoln only', *L.N.Q.* **5**, 1898, 99-104 & 107-12. List, medieval.

STENTON, DORIS M., ed. *The earliest Lincolnshire assize rolls, A.D. 1202-1209.* L.R.S. **22**. 1926.

STENTON, DORIS MARY, ed. *Rolls of the justices in eyre, being the rolls of pleas and assizes for Lincolnshire, 1218-9, and Worcestershire, 1221.* Publications of the Selden Society **53**. 1934.

THOMSON, WALTER SINCLAIR, ed. *A Lincolnshire assize roll for 1298 (P.R.O. assize roll no.505).* L.R.S. **36**. 1944. Includes list of royal officials, 1294-8, and an extensive biographical index.

WOOLGAR, C.M. 'A Lincolnshire coroner's roll', *L.H.A.* **16**, 1981, 13-17. 13th c.

HARDING, ALAN, ed. 'Early *trailbaston* proceedings from the Lincoln roll of 1305', in HUNNISETT, R.F., & POST, J.B., eds. *Medieval legal records edited in memory of C.A.F. Meekings.* H.M.S.O., 1978, 144-68.

McLANE, BERNARD WILLIAM, ed. *The 1341 royal inquest in Lincolnshire.* L.R.S. **78**. 1987.

'List of coroners rolls', *L.N.Q.* **5**, 1898, 112. 1342-96.

KIMBALL, ELISABETH G., ed. *Records of some sessions of the peace in the City of Lincoln, 1351-1354, and the Borough of Stamford, 1351.* L.R.S. **65**. 1971.

SILLEM, ROSAMUND, ed. *Records of some sessions of the peace in Lincolnshire, 1360-1375.* L.R.S. **30**. 1936.

KIMBALL, ELISABETH G., ed. *Records of some sessions of the peace in Lincolnshire, 1381-1396.* L.R.S. **49** & **56**. 1955-62. v.1. The Parts of Kesteven and the Parts of Holland. v.2. The Parts of Lindsey.

WELBY, ALFRED. 'Kesteven Grand Jury, 1450', *L.N.Q.* **7**, 1904, 227-8. Lists jurors.

LEADAM, I.S., ed. *The Domesday of inclosures, 1517-1518: being the extant returns to Chancery for Berks., Bucks., Cheshire, Essex, Leicestershire, Lincolnshire, Northants., Oxon., and Warwickshire, by the Commissioners of Inclosure in 1517, and for*

Bedfordshire in 1518, together with Dugdale's ms. notes on the Warwickshire inquisitions in 1517, 1518 and 1549. 2 vols. Longmans Green & Co., 1897. Names many landlords.

KIRKUS, A. MARY, & OWEN, A.E.B., eds. *The records of the Commissioners of Sewers in the Parts of Holland, 1547-1603.* L.R.S. **54, 63 & 71.** 1959-77. Includes biographical notes on commissioners. Sewers were waterways. Supplemented by:

KENNEDY, MARK E. 'Commissioners of Sewers for Lincolnshire, 1509-1649: an annotated list', *L.H.A.* **19,** 1984, 83-88.

MADDISON, A.R. 'List of Justices of the Peace for the Parts of Lindsey in Lincolnshire, A.D. 1626', *L.N.Q.* **4,** 1896, 181-4.

BINNALL, PETER B.G. 'The Commission of Array for Lincolnshire, 1642', *Local historian [Lincs]* **23,** 1939, 2-3. Lists Arraymen.

'Magistrates in the Fenland, 1650', *F.N.Q.* **2,** 1892-4, 46-7. List for Holland and Cambridgeshire.

WOOD, A.C. 'A list of Lincolnshire royalists, 1659', *L.A.A.S.R.P.* N.S. **1,** 1939, 217-9.

PEYTON, S.A., ed. *Minutes of proceedings in Quarter Sessions held for the Parts of Kesteven in the County of Lincoln, 1674-1695.* L.R.S. **25-6.** 1931.

'Lincolnshire justices, &c., 1693', *F.N.Q.* **5,** 1901-3, 386-92. List.

D[UDDING], R.C. 'Grand jurymen at Lincoln Assizes, 27 July 1800', *L.N.Q.* **19,** 1928, 58-9. List.

'County of Lincoln', in *Abstracts of the returns of charitable donations for the benefit of poor persons, made by the ministers and churchwardens of the several parishes and townships in England and Wales, 1786-1788.* House of Commons parliamentary papers, 1816, XVIA, 677-746. Names many benefactors, *etc.,* as do the following:

CHARITY COMMISSIONERS *Copies of the General digest of endowed charities ...: County of Lincoln.* House of Commons Parliamentary Paper, 1868-9, XLV, 333-461. Tables only.

CHARITY COMMISSIONERS *Report* ... W. Clowes and Sons, for H.M.S.O., 1839. 32nd report; part 4 covers Lincolnshire.

CHARITY COMMISSIONERS. *Return of the digest of endowed charities in the County of Lincoln* ... House of Commons Parliamentary papers, 1894, LXIII, 501-89. 1869. Tables only.

WICKSTEAD, ARTHUR. *Lincolnshire, Lindsey: the story of the County Council, 1889-1974.* Gainsborough: Lincolnshire and Humberside Arts, 1978. Includes a 'record of members', i.e. county councillors.

Poor law records are particularly useful to genealogist. For those in the Lincolnshire Archives Office, see:

LINCOLNSHIRE ARCHIVES OFFICE *Lists and indexes I: Poor Law Union records. A list of records covering poor law administration for 1834-c.1930.* Lincoln: Lincolnshire County Council, Recreational Services, 1992.

For a comprehensive index of Lincolnshire poor law documents, every genealogist should consult the important:

COLE, ANNE E., ed. *Lincolnshire poor law index.* 6 vols. [ ]: Society for Lincolnshire History and Archaeology Family History Committee/Lincolnshire Family History Society, 1987-91. Pt.1. Index to settlement certificates. Pt.2. Index to settlement examinations. Pt.3. Index to removal orders. Pt.4. Index to settlement papers in the Lindsey Quarter Session (2 vols.). Pt.5. Index to pauper apprenticeship indentures. Pt.6. Index to bastardy documents.

See also:

COLE, ANNE. 'The poor law index', *L.F.H.S.M.* **1** (4), 1990, 83-5. Brief description.

COLE, ANNE, ed. *Settlement examinations from the Kesteven Quarter Sessions, 1700-1847.* 5 fiche. Lincoln: L.F.H.S., 1993.

COLE, ANNE. 'Settlement papers in the Lindsey quarter sessions, 1732-1818', *S.L.H.A.F.H.S.N.* **5**(5), 1986, 10-11. Brief discussion.

COLE, ANNE, & MACKINDER, ALICE. *Lindsey petty sessions settlement examinations.* 3 fiche. Lincoln: L.F.H.S., 1992. Covers 1822-48.

15. RECORDS OF PAROCHIAL AND BOROUGH ADMINISTRATION

The records of parochial and borough government — the accounts of overseers, churchwardens and other parish officers, rate lists, burgess rolls, etc. — contain much information of genealogical value. They are listed here by parish, etc. Many parochial documents from throughout the county are listed in:

COMMITTEE FOR THE SURVEY OF PAROCHIAL DOCUMENTS WITHIN THE DIOCESE AND COUNTY OF LINCOLN. *Exhibition of parochial records held in the Usher Art Gallery, Lincoln, 14th June - 2nd July 1939.* The Committee, 1939.

Addlethorpe
DUDDING, REGINALD C. 'Addlethorpe and Ingoldmells churchwardens accounts', *L.N.Q.* 17, 1923, 151-80. Extracts, 16-17th c.

Aslackby
D[UDDING], R.C. 'An unusual vestry book', *L.N.Q.* 23, 1936, 45-53. Of Aslackby; 17th c. extract. Also includes list of incumbents, 1225-1906.

Billinghay
'Poor relief in Billinghay, 1828/9', *S.L.H.A.F.H.S.N.* 5(7), 1987, 16-17. Lists applicants for relief.

Boston
BAILEY, JOHN F., ed. *Transcription of minutes of the Corporation of Boston.* 5 vols. [Boston]: History of Boston Project, 1980-93. v.1. 1545 to 1607. v.2. 1608 to 1638. v.3. 1638 to 1671. v.4. 1671 to 1717. v.5. 1717-1763.

CLARK, PETER, & CLARK, JENNIFER, eds. *The Boston assembly minutes, 1545-1575.* L.R.S. 77. 1986.

RIGBY, S.H. 'Boston and Grimsby in the middle ages: an administrative contrast', *Journal of medieval history* 10, 1984, 51-66. Includes useful references.

Caistor Union
RAWDING, CHARLES. 'The Poor Law Amendment Act, 1834-1865: a case study of Caistor Poor Law Union', *L.H.A.* 22, 1987, 15-23.

Candleshoe Deanery
MADDISON, A.R. 'Churchwardens in the Deanery of Candleshoe, 1638', *L.N.Q.* 6, 1901, 89-90. List.

Castle Carlton
See North Reston

Deeping Fen
DACK, C. 'Deeping Fen', *F.N.Q.* 4, 1898-1900, 11-13. Includes list of those levied for drainage rates, 1744.

Deeping St.James
BURCHNALL, C.R. 'Deeping St.James parish constable's accounts', *Local historian [Lincs.]* 15-16, 1937, passim. 18th c.

SKENE, S.W. 'Assessment at Deeping St.James', *F.N.Q.* 6, 1904-6, 159. Mid-17th c. rate.

'Corpus Christi Guild at Deeping St.James', *F.N.Q.* 4, 1898-1900, 309-19. See also 392-3 & 5, 1901-3, 52. Accounts, 16th c.

Graffoe
TINLEY, RUTH. 'The Graffoe hiring statutes', *S.L.H.A. newsletter* 49, 1986, 8-9. Brief discussion of a 'hiring book', early 19th c., recording the hiring of servants.

Grantham
MARRAT, WILLIAM. *An historical description of Grantham, containing a list of the burgesses in Parliament, also of the succession of aldermen.* Lincoln: the author, 1816. Includes list of aldermen, 1430-1804.

WELBY, ALFRED C.E. 'The Hospital of Grantham', *L.N.Q.* 14, 1916-17, 17-20. Lists wardens or rectors, 1346-16th c., of this leper hospital.

Grimsby
GIBBONS, ALFRED. 'The records of the Corporation of Great Grimsby', in HISTORICAL MANUSCRIPTS COMMISSION. *Fourteenth report, appendix, part VIII: the manuscripts of Lincoln, Bury St.Edmunds and Great Grimsby corporation ...* C.7881. H.M.S.O., 1895, 237-91. Includes a list of mayors, 1202-1669.

Grimsby *continued*

BATES, ANDERSON. *A gossip about old Grimsby with a complete list of the mayors from the year 1202 to the present time, and the members of the Borough from 1639.* Grimsby: Albert Gait, 1893.

GILLETT, E.E. 'An early churchwardens' account of St.Marys, Grimsby', *L.A.A.S.R.P.* N.S. **5**, 1955-6, 27-36. 15th c.

'Grimsby burgess rolls, 29 Hen.VI-44 Eliz.', *N.G.* **1**, 1895, 1-4, 67-72, 140-41 & 225-6.

GREENFIELD, LILIAN. *Grimsby's freemen contrasted with the freemen of other towns.* Grimsby: Castle Press, 1950. General discussion.

Index to the Grimsby freemen's roll book. Grimsby: South Humberside Area Archive Office, 1992.

See also Boston

Gunby

'The town book of Gunby, A.D. 1588', *L.N.Q.* **7**, 1904, 237-49.

Haxey

NEILL, ERIC. *Some Haxey parish indexes.* Doncaster: Haxey & Westwoodside Heritage Society, 1989. Name index of victims of fire, 1744, enclosure award, 1803, tithe award, 1847, and road book, 1858.

'Fracas at Haxey Carr', *Islonian* **4**(5), 1993, 11-13. Includes list of defendants from Haxey in a Star Chamber case, 1595.

Heckington

S., H.T. *Notes on St.Andrew's church, Heckington, in the County of Lincoln, with extracts from the churchwardens accounts and parish registers.* Sleaford: J. Sewards, 1912.

Holbeach

MACDONALD, GRANT W. 'Holbeach parish records', *L.N.Q.* **4**, 1896, 66-71. Brief extracts, 18th c.

'Trespass at Holbeach, 1769', *F.N.Q.* **6**, 1903-6, 111-14. Includes list of 42 jurymen.

Horncastle

BOYD, WILLIAM K. 'Records of ancient Horncastle, 1086-1328', *L.N.Q.* **3**, 1893, 213-7 & 244-7; **4**, 1895, 16-18, 57-62, 116-20, 185-8, 217-21 & 234-8; **5**, 1898, 216-22 & 243-50.

Huttoft

D[UDDING], R.C. 'Huttoft churchwardens accounts', *L.N.Q.* **21**, 1931, 25-32. Extracts, 1688.

Ingoldmells

See Addlethorpe

Kirton in Lindsey

BINNALL, PETER B.G. 'The church account book and other records at Kirton in Lindsey', *Local historian* **3-7**, 1935-6, passim.

HOWLETT, ENGLAND. 'Burial in woollen', *Reliquary* N.S. **5**, 1891, 205-8. Includes affidavits from Kirton in Lindsey, Lincolnshire.

Leverton

DUDDING, REGINALD C. 'Leverton tithe book, A.D. 1754', *L.N.Q.* **19**, 1928, 24-7. Brief extracts.

PEACOCK, EDWARD. 'Extracts from the churchwardens' accounts of the parish of Leverton, in the county of Lincoln', *Archaeologia* **41**(2), 1867, 333-70. Includes names.

Lincoln

BIRCH, WALTER DE GRAY. *Catalogue of the royal charters and other documents, and list of books belonging to the Corporation of Lincoln, now preserved in the muniment room of the Corporation.* 2 vols. Lincoln: City of Lincoln, 1904-6. Extensive list of archives.

BIRCH, WALTER DE GRAY. 'City of Lincoln: catalogue of the royal charters and other documents belonging to the Corporation ...', *L.N.Q.* **10**, 1909, 88-95, 107-18, 150-56, 167-77, 218-23 & 250-55; **11**, 1911, 19-26, 94-6 & 123-8.

MACRAY, WILLIAM DUNN. 'The manuscripts of the Corporation of Lincoln', in HISTORICAL MANUSCRIPTS COMMISSION. *Fourteenth report, appendix, part VIII: the manuscripts of Lincoln, Bury St.Edmunds and Great Grimsby corporations ...* C.7881. H.M.S.O., 1895, 1-120.

Names of the mayors, bailiffs, sheriffs and chamberlains of the City of Lincoln since the year of our Lord 1313 ... Lincoln: John Drury, [1787?]

Lincoln continued

HILL, J.W.F. 'Three lists of the mayors, bailiffs and sheriffs of Lincoln', *A.A.S.R.P.* **39**, 1929, 217-56.

F., F.R. 'The Leper Hospital of the Holy Innocents, without Lincoln', *L.N.Q.* **8**, 1905, 230-32. Includes list of wardens, 1284-1345.

Lissington

'Inventory of records at the church of St.John the Baptist, Lissington', *Local historian [Lincs]* **13**, 1937, 4.

Louth

GOULDING, R.W. *Louth old corporation records, being extracts from the accounts, minutes and memoranda of the warden and six assistants of the town of Louth and free school of King Edward VI in Louth, and other ancient documents relating to the town.* Louth: J.W. Goulding, 1891. Includes list of wardens, 1551-1878.

DUDDING, REGINALD C., ed. *The first churchwardens' book of Louth, 1500-1524.* Oxford: O.U.P., 1941.

BANKS, SIR JOSEPH. 'Extracts out of an old book relating to the building of Louth steeple, and repairing the church, &c., from about the year 1500 or 1501 to 1518', *Archaeologia* **10**, 1792, 70-98. Accounts, giving many names.

A valuation of all the messuages, tenements, lands and property, situate in the parish of Louth, in the County of Lincoln, rated for the relief of the poor, made and taken pursuant to orders of the select vestry. Louth: Henry Hurton, 1823. Re-issued on microfiche as *Louth valuation 1823.* [Lincoln]: L.F.H.S., [199-?]

North Hykeham

'Records of North and South Hykeham', *Local historian [Lincs]* **12**, 1937, 4. List of parish records.

North Reston

'North Reston, South Reston and Castle Carlton', *Local historian [Lincs]* **15**, 1937, 4. List of parish records.

Saxilby

GIBBONS, A. 'A transcription of the old churchwardens accounts of the parish of Saxilby', *A.A.S.R.P.* **19**, 1888, 376-90. Covers 1551-1665, with gaps, and 1746.

Scothorne

ALLISON, H.F. 'Scothorne churchwardens accounts', *L.N.Q.* **11**, 1911, 70-76. Brief extracts, 1585-91.

Sleaford

TINLEY, RUTH, MACKINDER, ALICE, & COLE, ANNE. *Sleaford petty sessions settlement examinations.* 1 fiche. Lincoln: L.F.H.S., 1993. 1829-35.

'Computus of the Holy Trinity Guild of Sleaford', *L.N.Q.* **23**, 1936, 91-7. Extracts, 1477.

South Hykeham

See North Hykeham

South Reston

See North Reston

Spalding

'Fire at Spalding, 1715', *F.N.Q.* **3**, 1895-7, 338-47. Lists contributors to the relief fund, etc.

'Spalding fireworks, 1749', *F.N.Q.* **3**, 1895-7, 362-7. Includes list of subscribers to fireworks display in celebration of the Treaty of Aix-La-Chapelle.

Stamford

HARTLEY, J.S. 'Death by misadventure: coroners' inquests in Stamford, 1700-1850', *Stamford historian* **2**, 1978, 7-20. General discussion.

Strubby

DUDDING, REGINALD C. 'Two Strubby parish books, 1571-1653. *L.N.Q.* **15**, 1919, 212-8 & 249-56; **16**, 1921, 29-32 & 69-75.

Sutterton

PEACOCK, EDWARD. 'Churchwardens' accounts of Saint Mary's, Sutterton', *Archaeological journal* **39**, 1882, 53-63. 15-16th c.

Tetford

D[UDDING], R.C. 'Tetford account book', *L.N.Q.* **23**, 1936, 39-42. Brief extracts, 18-19th c.

Wigtoft

[NICHOLS, JOHN.] *Illustrations of the manners and expences of antient times in England, in the fifteenth, sixteenth and seventeenth centuries, deduced from the accompts of churchwardens and other authentic documents, collected from various parts of the Kingdom.* The author, 1797. See 77-84 and 195-249 for abstracts from the 15th c. Wigtoft churchwardens' accounts.

Willoughton

P., M. 'A constable's accounts for the parish of Willoughton, 1757', *L.N.Q.* **5**, 1898, 40-42. See also 61-2.

16. ESTATE RECORDS

A. *General*

The records of estate administration constitute a mine of information of the genealogist. Much is in print, although much more lies untouched in the archives. Most of the medieval feet of fines, that is, deeds, have been abstracted; these are a vital source of information on landowners. See:

WALKER, MARGARET S., ed. *Feet of fines for the County of Lincoln for the reign of King John, 1199-1216.* Publications of the Pipe Roll Society **67**; N.S. **29**. 1954. This partially supersedes:

BOYD, W., & MASSINGBERD, W.O. *Lincolnshire records: abstracts of final concords, temp. Richard I, John, and Henry III.* 2 vols. Spottiswoode & Co., 1896. Described as vol.1., pts 1-2. Many inaccuracies. Continued in:

FOSTER, C.W., ed. *Final concords of the County of Lincoln from the feet of fines preserved in the Public Record Office, A.D. 1244-1272, with additions from various sources, A.D. 1176-1250. Vol. II.* L.R.S. **17**. 1920.

BOYD, W. 'Feet of fines ...', *L.N.Q.* **3**, 1893, 91-3, 119-22, 149-51, 180-82 & 201-3; **4**, 1896, 21-3; **6**, 1901, 164-72, 218-24 & 235-44; **7**, 1904, 8-16, 40-50, 92-5, 108-16, 132-47, 184-92, 206-10 & 249-55; **8**, 1905, 20-30, 43-6, 88-95, 124-8 & 189-91.

Lincolnshire deeds enrolled on the Close Rolls are calendared in:

BOYD, W. 'Calendar of all enrolments on the Close Rolls, *temp.* Henry VII, relating to the county of Lincoln', *A.A.S.R.P.* **23**(2), 1896, 260-73.

Many 12th c. deeds relating to Lincolnshire, Nottinghamshire, Derbyshire, Leicestershire and Rutland are abstracted in:

STENTON, F.M., ed. *Documents illustrative of the social and economic history of the Danelaw from various collections.* Records of the social and economic history of England and Wales **5**. Oxford University Press for the British Academy, 1920.

There are a number of calendars, *etc.,* of deeds from Lincolnshire in general:

HALL, T. WALTER. *A descriptive catalogue of ancient charters & instruments relating to lands near Sheffield in the counties of York, Derby, Nottingham & Lincoln, with genealogies & notes.* Sheffield: J.W. Northend, 1935.
'The value of old parchment documents in genealogical and topographical research', *Genealogical quarterly* **4**, 1935-6, 146-60. Lincolnshire deed abstracts.

BLOOM, J.H. 'Abstracts of Lincolnshire deeds', *L.N.Q.* **8**, 1905, 201-10 & 233-41; **9**, 1907, 3-15, 41-9 & 90-95. Relating to Helpringham, Tothill, Gayton, Thorpe Latimer, Bicker, Ropley, Reston, Algarkirk, Fossdyke, Gayton, Withern and Scredington.
'Some 14th century Lincolnshire deeds', *L.N.Q.* **18**, 1925, 60-69, 88-92, 103-8, 120-26, 139-43 & 157-9. Abstracts from an antiquarian collection.

For a brief list of Lincolnshire court rolls, see: GIBBONS, ALFRED, & FOSTER, W.E. 'Lincolnshire court rolls', *L.N.Q.* **1**, 1889, 44-6 & 209-10.

B. *Private Estates*
The larger proprietors of Lincolnshire had lands in various parts of the county, and sometimes in other counties as well. The estate papers of a number of families have been listed and published; these and other works on private estates are entered here.

Boston
HARDY, W.J. *The Rt. Hon. Lord Boston's muniments at Hedsor relating to South Lincolnshire*, ed. W.E. Foster. Horncastle: W.K. Morton & Sons, 1914. Abstracts of 207 deeds, *etc.* reprinted from *L.N.Q.* **13**, 1914, 9-30, 51-63, 78-93, 105-27 & 158-60. Mainly concerning Moulton.

Brownlow
JOHNSON, C.P.C. 'The Brownlow manuscripts', *L.F.H.S.M.* **3**(4), 1992, 140-41. Brief description of estate records which includes records from over 75 places in Lincolnshire.

Chester
BARRACLOUGH, GEOFFREY., ed. *The charters of the Norman Earls of Chester c.1071-1237.* Record Society of Lancashire and Chester, 1988. Includes much Lincolnshire material.

Cony
TURNOR, EDMUND. 'Extracts from the household-book of Thomas Cony of Bassingthorpe, c.Lincoln', *Archaeologia* **11**, 1794, 22-33. Includes rental, 1577, of lands in Lincolnshire and Rutland, naming bailiffs.

Dalison
'Dalison notes: abstracts of deeds from the Elkington Hall muniment room', *M.G.H.* 2nd series **2**, 1888, 129-30, 153-4, 165-6, 184-7, 198, 232-3, 241-4, 257-9, 289-90, 346, 353-4 & 381-2. Of Northamptonshire, Lincolnshire, *etc.* Deeds, inquisitions post mortem, court records, letters, *etc.*, mainly medieval.

Heneage
HILL, J.W.F., ed. 'Sir George Heneage's estate book, 1625', *L.A.A.S.R.P.* N.S. **1**, 1939, 35-84 & 177-216. Relates to Hainton, East Barkwith, Sixhill, South Willingham, Benniworth, Ludford, Withcall, Tathwell, Stewton, Saltfleetby and Grainthorpe, and to the Wellow Abbey lands.

Lumley
BEASTALL, T.W. *A North County estate: the Lumleys and Saundersons as landowners, 1600-1900.* Phillimore & Co., 1975. General account of estate management in Co.Durham, Lincolnshire and Yorkshire.

Massingberd
MAJOR, KATHLEEN. 'The Massingberd deeds and papers at Gunby Hall, Spilsby', *L.A.A.S.R.P.* N.S. **3**, 1945, 8-11. Brief description.

Saunderson
See Lumley

C. *Ecclesiastical Estates*
Ecclesiastical estates were of great importance, especially prior to the Reformation; further, their records had a much greater chance of survival than the records of private families, since they were 'perpetual' institutions. Their deeds were frequently collected together into chartularies, many of which have been published. These, together with other ecclesiastical estate records, are listed here. There are two works dealing with the estate records of particular religious orders throughout Lincolnshire:

STENTON, F.M., ed. *Transcripts of charters relating to the Gilbertine houses of Sixle, Ormsby, Catley, Bullington, and Alvingham.* L.R.S. **18**. 1922.

FINCHAM, H.W. 'An index to Hospitallers properties in Great Britain', *L.N.Q.* **16**, 1921, 138-56. List of deeds, *etc.* relating to the Order of St.John of Jerusalem in Lincolnshire.

Alvingham Priory
GOULDING, R.W. 'Alvingham Priory book', *L.N.Q.* **3**, 1893, 183-6. See also **4**, 1896, 85-7.

Bardney Abbey
'Three Bardney charters, temp XIII century', *L.N.Q.* **5**, 1898, 81-4.
See also section 9B above.

Burwell Priory
TRABAT-CUSSAC, J.P. 'Les Possessions Anglaises de l'Abbaye de la Sauve-Majeure: le prieuré de Burwell (Lincolnshire)', *Bulletin philologique et historique* ... 1957 (1958), 137-83. Includes list of priors, and notes on manorial lords of Burwell, 1086-1545. In French.

Crowland Abbey
GOUGH, R. *The history and antiquities of Croyland Abbey in the County of Lincoln,* in Bibliotheca topographica Britannica **3**. J. Nichols, 1790. Includes many deed abstracts.
PAGE, FRANCES M. *The estates of Crowland Abbey: a study in manorial organisation.* Cambridge: C.U.P., 1934. Includes deed abstracts, *etc.,* for manors in Cambridgeshire, Lincolnshire, Huntingdonshire and Northamptonshire.
RABAN, SANDRA. *The estates of Thorney and Crowland: a study in medieval monastic land tenure.* Occasional paper **7**. Cambridge: University of Cambridge Dept. of Land Economy, 1977.
See also Spalding Priory

Gokewell
LOWE, F. PYNDAR. 'On some charters relating to the nunnery of Gokewell in Lincolnshire', *A.A.S.R.P.* **3**(1), 1854, 102-8. 12th c.
L., L.B. 'Charters relating to the family of De Alta Ripa, and nunnery of Gokewell,

Co.Lincoln', *Collectanea topographica et genealogica* **4**, 1837, 241-2. 12th c.

Haverholme Priory
'Haverholme Priory charters', *L.N.Q.* **17**, 1923, 7-48, 65-74 & 89-98. Calendar of 203 deeds, with detailed index.

Kirkstead Abbey
OWEN, DOROTHY M. 'A Kirkstead Abbey valuation of 1537', *L.H.A.* **24**, 1989, 41-5. Includes names of tenants.

Lincoln Cathedral
FOSTER, C.W., *et al,* eds. *The registrum antiquissimum of the Cathedral church of Lincoln.* L.R.S. **27-9, 32, 34, 41-2, 51, 62 & 67-8.** 1931-73. Chartulary, with innumerable deeds, and notes on family of Condel (in v.27) on the Alselin and Caux estates (in v.46), and on 13th c. mayors and bailiffs of Lincoln (v.51).
MASSINGBERD, W.O. 'Lincoln Cathedral charters', *A.A.S.R.P.* **26**(1), 1901, 18-96; **26**(2), 1902, 321-69; **27**(1), 1903, 1-91. Medieval.
SALTER, H.E. 'The charters of Henry I and Stephen at Lincoln Cathedral', *English historical review* **23**, 1908, 725-8. Abstracts of 9 12th c. deeds.
SALTER, HERBERT E. 'Charters of Henry II at Lincoln Cathedral', *English historical review* **24**, 1909, 303-13. Abstracts of 35 12th c. charters.
GALBRAITH, V.H. 'Seven charters of Henry II at Lincoln Cathedral', *Antiquaries journal* **12**, 1932, 269-78. Discussion of, and notes on, charters mentioned in the *Registrum antiquissimum.*

Lincoln Diocese
JENSEN, G.F. 'The names of the Lincolnshire tenants of the Bishop of Lincoln, c.1225', in SANDGREN, F., ed. *Otium et negotium: studies in onomatology and library science presented to Olof Von Feilitzen.* Acta Bibliotheca Regia Stockholmiensis **16**. Stockholm: Kungliga Biblioteket, 1932, 86-95.

Peterborough Abbey
MELLOWS, W.T. 'The estates of the monastery of Peterborough in the County of Lincoln', *L.H.* **1**(3), 1948, 100-114; **1**(4), 1949, 128-66. General discussion, identifying sources; the estates were mainly in the Liberty of Scotter.

Peterborough Abbey *continued*

ROFFE, DAVID. 'The *descriptio terrarum* of Peterborough Abbey', *Historical research* **65**, 1992, 1-16. Lists Lincolnshire lands of this Northamptonshire abbey.

Ramsey Abbey
BIRCH, W. DE G. 'Historical notes on the manuscripts belonging to Ramsey Abbey', *Journal of the British Archaeological Association* N.S. **5**, 1899, 229-42. Ramsey Abbey, Huntingdonshire; includes notes on Lincolnshire properties.

Revesby Abbey
STANHOPE, EDWARD. *Abstracts of the deeds and charters relating to Revesby Abbey, 1142-1539*. Horncastle: W.K. Morton, 1889.

Sempringham Priory
FOSTER, C.W. 'Grants to Sempringham Priory by members of the Langton family', *A.A.S.R.P.* **37**(2), 1925, 241-6. Deeds, with 12-13th c. pedigree.
'Charters relating to the Priory of Sempringham', *Genealogist* N.S. **15**, 1899, 158-61 & 221-7; **16**, 1900, 30-35, 76-83, 153-8 & 223-8; **17**, 1901, 29-35, 164-8 & 232-9.

Spalding Priory
HALLAM, H.E. 'Age at first marriage and age at death in the Lincolnshire Fenland, 1252-1478', *Population studies* **39**, 1985, 55-69. Based on Spalding Priory and Crowland Abbey estate records.
JONES, E.D. 'Going round in circles: some new evidence for population in the later middle ages', *Journal of medieval history* **15**(4), 1989, 329-45. See also 347-58, & **17**, 1991, 263-9. General discussion based on the 'Myntling' register, which gives pedigrees of hundreds of Spalding Priory tenants, c.1470. Includes pedigrees of Sutton and Drake.
JONES, E.D. 'Villein mobility in the later middle ages: the case of Spalding Priory', *Nottingham medieval studies* **36**, 1992, 151-66. Based on the 'Myntling' register.

Thornton Abbey
CRAGG, W.A. 'Rental of estates of Thornton Abbey', *L.N.Q.* **10**, 1909, 136-42. 1604(?)

D. *Records of Particular Places*

Addlethorpe
See Ingoldmells

Algarkirk
FORDHAM, PAUL. 'The acre books of Algarkirk-cum-Fosdike', *L.H.* **2**(1), 1954, 7-12. Discussion, not a transcript.

Anderby
DUDDING, REGINALD C. 'A survey of Anderby and Cumberworth', *L.N.Q.* **23**, 1936, 62-9.

Aslackby
DUDDING, REGINALD C. 'Some Aslackby deeds', *L.N.Q.* **23**, 1936, 133-46. Abstracts, 16-17th c.

Bayeux
'Survey of the Barony of Bayeux, A.D. 1288', *L.N.Q.* **8**, 1905, 46-61 & 75-88.

Bottesford
PEACOCK, EDWARD. 'Notes from the records of the manor of Bottesford, Lincolnshire', *Archaeologia* **50**(2), 1887, 371-82. Includes many names from 16th c. court rolls.

Bourne
VENABLES, EDMUND. 'Bourne: its castle and its abbey', *A.A.S.R.P.* **20**(1), 1889, 1-19. Includes extracts from 16th c. account, giving some names; also a few deeds, *etc.*
'Manors of Bourne and Deeping', *F.N.Q.* **7**, 1907-9, 236-8. Six deeds from the Patent Rolls, 14th c.

Burgh
MASSINGBERD, W.O. 'Holles estate in Burgh', *L.N.Q.* **10**, 1909, 211-13. Deed abstracts, 16-18th c.

Cabourne
See Steeping

Coningsby
'Conyngesby (now Coneysby) compotus roll, A.D. 1431', *L.N.Q.* **12**, 1912, 70-6.

Crowland
'[Croyland manor amercements]', *L.N.Q.* **13**, 1914, 101-5. Brief extracts, 1727-35.

Cumberworth
See Anderby

Deeping
See Bourne

Denton
See Harlaxton

Digby
HOSFORD, W.H. 'Digby in 1801: the anatomy of a Lincolnshire village', *L.H.* 2(3), 1957, 26-33. Includes list of tenants of Lord Harrowby, 1801, *etc.*

Doddington
PORTES, WM. 'Doddington estate accounts, 1788-1791', *L.N.Q.* 14, 1916-17, 216-24 & 251-5; 15, 1919, 27-32, 59-64, 94-6, 175-8, 221-4 & 245-9; 16, 1921, 21-9, 51-64, 75-80 & 156-60; 17, 1923, 57-60 & 85-7. See also 149-50. Delaval family estate; many names of tenants.

East Kirkby
GOULDING, R.W. 'East Kirkby', *L.N.Q.* 5, 1898, 71-5. Abstracts of 13 medieval deeds.

Epworth
JACKSON, CHARLES. 'Notes from the court-rolls of the manor of Epworth, in the county of Lincoln', *Reliquary* 23, 1882-3, 44-8, 89-92 & 174-6. 16-18th c.

Fleet
NEILSON, N., ed. *A terrier of Fleet, Lincolnshire, from a manuscript in the British Museum.* Records of social and economic history 4. Oxford University Press for the British Academy, 1920. c.1316.

Fosdyke
See Algarkirk

Gosberton
'Gosberton court rolls', *N.G.* 2, 1896, 85-6. Brief medieval extracts.

Grayingham
MADDISON, A.R. 'Manors of Grayingham and Waddingham', *L.N.Q.* 10, 1909, 126-8. Abstracts of 16 deeds, 15-17th c.

Harlaxton
WELBY, ALFRED C.E. 'Deeds at Harlaxton: families of Denton, Upton, Williams', *L.N.Q.* 12, 1912, 121-5 & 154-60. Abstracts of deeds concerning Harlaxton, Denton, Wyville, Hungerton and area, 13-14th c.

Haugh
DUDDING, REGINALD C. 'Some Haugh deeds', *L.N.Q.* 21, 1931, 113-8; 22, 1934, 8-14 & 27-30. 17-18th c.

Heighington
EAST, F.W., ed. 'The Heighington terrier', *L.A.A.S.R.P.* N.S. 4, 1951, 131-63 & 5, 1953, 28-69. Full survey of the entire parish, 1575; recording all holdings. Many names.

Hibaldstow
L., B.L. 'Charters relating to the lands of the Priory of Newstead in Cadney, at Hibaldstow in Lincolnshire', *Collectanea topographica et genealogica* 5, 1838, 157-60.
MADDISON, A.R. 'Court rolls of the manor of Hibaldstow', *L.N.Q.* 7, 1904, 35-40. 14-17th c., brief extracts.
PEACOCK, E. 'The court rolls of the manor of Hibaldstow', *Archaeological journal* 44, 1887, 278-88. 15-16th c.

Humberstone
'Terrier of land at Humberstone', *L.N.Q.* 18, 1925, 41-6. 1686.

Hungerton
WELBY, ALFRED C.E. 'Harlaxton deeds: manors of Hungerton and Wyville', *L.N.Q.* 12, 1912, 233-6. Abstracts, 15-16th c.
See also Harlaxton

Ingoldmells
MASSINGBERD, W.O., ed. *Court rolls of the manor of Ingoldmells in the County of Lincoln.* Spottiswoode & Co., 1902. 13-16th c.
MADDISON, A.R. 'Manor of Ingoldmells-cum-Addlethorpe court rolls', *A.A.S.R.P.* 21, 1891, 176-90. Medieval.
'Some accounts of the manor of Ingoldmells', *L.N.Q.* 7, 1904, 157-60, 167-78 & 203-4. 14-15th c.

Kettlethorpe

JARVIS, EDWIN GEORGE. 'Documents relating to the family of Swynford, from the Kettlethorpe title-deeds of Colonel Cracroft-Amcotts', *Archaeological journal* 21, 1864, 254-9. Medieval deeds.

Killingholme

See Steeping

Langton

MASSINGBERD, W.O. 'Some ancient records relating to the manor of Langton and its lords', *A.A.S.R.P.* 22(2), 1894, 157-73. Includes inquisitions post mortem of Langton family, various lists of fees, extents, deeds, *etc.*

Leake

DUDDING, REGINALD C. 'Conington mss', *L.N.Q.* 21, 1931, 107-12. Conington family deeds concerning properties in Leake, 16-17th c.

Lincoln

EXLEY, C.L. 'The leet or manorial court of the Cathedral church of Lincoln', *L.H.* 1, 1947-53, 307-12. Includes transcript of court roll, 1664.

HILL, J.W.F. 'The manor of Hungate, or Beaumont Fee, in the city of Lincoln', *A.A.S.R.P.* 38(1927), 175-208, Includes transcripts of many lists of names from manorial records, 17-18th c.

Long Bennington

D[UDDING], R.C. 'Court roll of Long Bennington', *L.N.Q.* 21, 1931, 21-4. 1417.

Lusby

'Bek of Lusby', *L.N.Q.* 6, 1901, 120-7 & 135-6. Mainly deed abstracts.

Nettleham

COTTON-SMITH, H., & LEWIS, F.C. 'Inventory of documents relating to Nettleham, in possession of Mrs A. Porter', *Local historian [Lincs]* 8, 1936, 4; 9, 1936, 4.

North Kelsey

DUDDING, REGINALD C. 'Two account rolls of the manor of North Hall in North Kelsey from the muniments of Sidney Sussex College, Cambridge', *L.N.Q.* 17, 1923, 128-30. Account of 1465.

Scotter

PEACOCK, EDWARD. 'Notes from the court rolls of the manor of Scotter', *Archaeologia* 46, 1881, 371-88. 16-17th c. extracts, with names.

Sleaford

HOSFORD, W.H. 'The manor of Sleaford in the thirteenth century', *Nottingham medieval studies* 12, 1968, 21-39. Based on a 13th c. survey; few names.

Somersby

MASSINGBERD, W.O. 'The manors of Somersby and Tetford', *A.A.S.R.P.* 23(2), 1896, 253-9. Deeds and inquisitions post mortem, mainly relating to the Thimbleby family.

South Elkington

MADDISON, A.R. 'Smyth mss deeds', *L.N.Q.* 11, 1911, 242-55. Abstracts of deeds relating to South Elkington and the surrounding area.

Spalding

HALLAM, H.E. 'The agrarian history of South Lincolnshire in the mid-fifteenth century', *Nottingham medieval studies* 11, 1967, 86-95. Includes name of Spalding tenants from 1478/9 manorial accounts.

Stallingborough

MADDISON, A.R. 'The manor of Stallingborough', *A.A.S.R.P.* 23(2), 1896, 274-89. Rental, 1351.

Stamford

COLES, KEN. '31 St.Paul's Street', *Stamford historian* 3, 1979, 15-21. Abstracts of 17 deeds, 18-19th c.

HARTLEY, JOHN S., & ROGERS, ALAN. *The religious foundations of medieval Stamford.* Stamford survey group report 2. Nottingham: University of Nottingham Dept. of Adult Education, 1974. Detailed discussion of ecclesiastical properties in the town.

'Some Stamford deeds', *F.N.Q.* 7, 1907-9, 379-81. Abstracts of five 17-18th c. deeds.

Steeping
SMITH, W.H. 'Inhabitants of Lincolnshire villages in the 16th century', *L.N.Q.* **5**, 1898, 19-23, 34-5 & 51-2. Extracts from Duchy of Lancaster court rolls for Steeping, Cabourne, Whitton and Killingholme.

Stickney
OWEN, DOROTHY M. 'Some Revesby charters of the Soke of Bolingbroke', in BARNES, PATRICIA M., & SLADE, C.F., eds. *A medieval miscellany for Doris Mary Stenton.* Publications of the Pipe Roll Society **76**; N.S. **36**, 1962, 221-34. 12th c. Revesby deeds relating to Stickney.

Stow
MASSINGBERD, W.O. 'Survey of the manor of Stow, A.D. 1283', *A.A.S.R.P.* **24**(2), 1898, 299-347.
VARLEY, JOAN. 'Some records of the manor of Stow', *L.A.A.S.R.P.* N.S. **4**, 1951, 68-79. Includes list of records, 17-19th c.

Swineshead. The Moor
'The manor of the Moor, Swineshead', *F.N.Q.* **3**, 1895-7, 25-8, 42-5, 76-8 & 223-4. Extracts from 17-18th c. court rolls.

Tetford
See Somersby

Threckingham
DUDDING, REGINALD C. 'Threckingham court roll', *L.N.Q.* **22**, 1934, 17-18. 1701-5 extracts.

Uffington
DUDDING, REGINALD C. 'The manor of Uffington', *L.N.Q.* **19**, 1928, 6-16. Account rolls, 1413/14 and 1454/5.

Ulceby
'[Terrier of Ulceby, 1707]', *L.N.Q.* **14**, 1916-17, 72-8.

Waddingham
See Grayingham

Whitton
See Steeping

Wyville
See Harlaxton

Wywell
WELBY, ALFRED C.E. 'Harlaxton deeds: Belvoir Priory property', *L.N.Q.* **12**, 1912, 221-2. Abstracts of deeds concerning Wywell, medieval.

E. *Manorial and Other Descents*
The descents of numerous manors have been traced; many are given in some of the antiquarian works listed above, section 1. Brief descents are also given in:
LEACH, TERENCE R. *Lincolnshire country houses and their families.* 2 vols. Dunholme: Laece, 1990-91.
LEACH, TERENCE R., & PACEY, ROBERT. *Lost Lincolnshire country houses.* 4 vols. Burgh Le Marsh: Old Chapel Lane Books, 1990-3. Gives descents of many properties.

Bag Enderby
See Somersby

Bilsby
DUDDING, REGINALD C. 'Abstract of title to an estate at Bilsby', *L.N.Q.* **20**, 1929, 113-21. Descent, 17-19th c.

Bonby
MADDISON, A.R. 'Bonby manor in the 14th and 15th centuries', *L.N.Q.* **10**, 1909, 2-11. Descent; includes pedigrees of Despenser, King, Rugeley, *etc.*

Brant Broughton
WELBY, ALFRED. 'Brant Broughton', *L.N.Q.* **15**, 1919, 82-94. Descent; includes pedigrees of Flaald, 12th c., and Daubeney, 11-14th c.

Bratoft
MASSINGBERD, W.O. 'Some lords of a manor in Bratoft', *L.N.Q.* **7**, 1904, 116-22. Medieval descent; includes pedigrees of Braytoft, Cressy and Markham.

Burgh
'An abstract of title', *L.N.Q.* **19**, 1928, 88-95. Title to land in Burgh, giving descent, 18th c.

Burwell
GOULDING, R.W. 'Notes on the lords of the manor of Burwell', *A.A.S.R.P.* **24**(1), 1897, 62-94. Descent of manor, 11-19th c., through Haye, Kyme, Cromwell, Brandon, Glemham and Lister.

Denton
WELBY, ALFRED C.E. 'Manor of Denton', *L.N.Q.* **9**, 1907, 229-32. See also **10**, 1909, 213-5. Medieval descent.

Driby
MASSINGBERD, W.O. 'Lords of the manor of Driby', *A.A.S.R.P.* **23**(1), 1895, 106-34. Includes many extracts from deeds, inquisitions post mortem, *etc.,* concerning the families of Driby, Bernak, and Cromwell; medieval.

East Barkwith
BINNALL, PETER B.G. 'Descent of lands in East and West Barkwith, Co.Lincoln', *L.A.A.S.R.P.* N.S. **3**, 1945, 138-43. Medieval.

Fulstow
WILLIAMSON, D.M. 'Some notes on the mediaeval manors of Fulstow', *L.A.A.S.R.P.* N.S. **4**, 1951, 1-56. Descent; includes some deed abstracts.

Greetwell
MADDISON, A.R. 'The manor of Greetwell', *L.N.Q.* **10**, 1909, 73-5. Medieval descent.

Irnham
TRAPPES-LOMAX, THOMAS BYRNAND. 'The owners of Irnham Hall, Co.Lincoln, and their contribution to the survival of Catholicism in that county', *L.A.A.S.R.P.* N.S. **9**, 1961, 164-77. Descent through Thimelby, Conquest, Clifford, *etc.*

Lincoln
JONES, STANLEY, MAJOR, KATHLEEN, & VARLEY, JOAN. *The survey of ancient houses in Lincoln.* 3 vols. 11 microfiche. Lincoln: Lincoln Civic Trust, 1984-90. v.1. Priorygate to Pottergate. v.2. Houses to the south and west of the Minster. v.3. Houses in Eastgate, Priorygate and James Street. Archaeological survey naming many occupants.

Mumby
DUDDING, REGINALD C. 'An abstract of title', *L.N.Q.* **18**, 1925, 32-40. To land at Mumby; much information on descent and on Hutton, Wallis, Poplar and Thornton families, *etc.,* 18-19th c.

Nocton
NORGATE, KATE, & FOOTMAN, MAURICE HENRY. 'Some notes for a history of Nocton', *A.A.S.R.P.* **24**(2), 1897, 347-81. Includes pedigrees showing descent of manor from Darcy to Lymbury, Wymbishe, Towneley, Stanhope, Ellys, Bourke, and Robinson; also lists of vicars and priors, and extracts from the parish registers.

Osgodby
MASSINGBERD, W.O. 'The manor of Osgodby', *L.N.Q.* **8**, 1905, 117-21. Descent, 11-13th c.

Pinchbeck
'Coxells Mill at Pinchbeck", *L.F.H.S.M.* **3**(2), 1992, 70-72. Traces owners, 18-20th c.

Potter Hanworth
MASSINGBERD, W.O. 'The manor of Potterhanworth', *L.N.Q.* **8**, 1905, 11-18 & 227-9. Medieval descent.

Saleby
DUDDING, REGINALD C. *History of the manor and parish of Saleby with Thoresthorpe in the County of Lincoln, with some owners.* Horncastle: W.K. Morton & Sons, 1922. Includes manorial descent.

Sedgebrook
WELBY, ALFRED. 'Sedgebrook manor, 1086-1772', *L.N.Q.* **20**, 1929, 70-72. Descent.

Somersby
LEACH, TERENCE R. 'The Somersby and Bag Enderby estate', *L.P.P.* **8**, 1992, 21-6. Descent, 16-19th c.

Stamford
TILL, E.C. 'St.Cuthberts Fee in Stamford', *Stamford historian* **6**, 1982, 29-34. Manorial descent, 16-18th c.
TILL, E.C. '19, St.George's Square, Stamford', *Stamford historian* **1**, 1977, 21-7. See also **2**, 1978, 23-7. Descent, 17-20th c., includes pedigree of Wigmore, 17-18th c.

Swinhope
MASSINGBERD, W.O. 'Some notes on the early history of the manor of Swinhope', *L.N.Q.* **10**, 1909, 66-73. Medieval descent, includes pedigree of Chauncy, 13-15th c.

Thoresthorpe
See Saleby

Waddingworth
FLETCHER, W.G. DIMOCK. 'The manor of Waddingworth, Co.Lincoln', *Reliquary* **15**, 1874-5, 72. Descent of manor, 1599-1746, through Goodrich, Townshend, Dymocke and Southwell.

Welby
WELBY, ALFRED C. 'Manor of Welby', *L.N.Q.* **10**, 1909, 48-51. Descent.

West Barkwith
See East Barkwith

F. *Enclosure Records*
Lincolnshire boasts an extraordinary number of detailed studies of enclosure — mostly from the pen of Rex Russell. Most of the works listed below include listings of local landowners named in enclosure awards. An overview of the subject — now rather dated — is provided by:
BECKWITH, I.S. 'The present state of enclosure studies in Lincolnshire: a bibliography of recent writing on enclosure in Lincolnshire', *Bulletin of local history: East Midlands Region* **6**, 1971, 21-37. Bibliographical essay.
See also:
RUSSELL, ELEANOR, & RUSSELL, REX C. *Parliamentary enclosure and new landscapes in Lincolnshire.* Lincolnshire history series **10**. Lincoln: Lincolnshire County Council Recreational Services, Libraries, 1987. Gives names of landowners from 37 enclosure awards.
LYONS, NICK, ed. *Enclosure in context in North-West Lincolnshire, part 1: commentary and documents.* Scunthorpe: Scunthorpe Borough Museum, 1988. The documents give many names.

HOSFORD, W.H. 'Some Lincolnshire enclosure documents', *Economic history review* 2nd series **2**(1), 1949, 73-9. Discussion of documents found in a solicitor's office.

Alkborough
RUSSELL, REX C. *The enclosures of Alkborough, 1765-1768, West Halton, 1772-1773, Whitton, 1773-1775, Scotter and Scotterthorpe, 1808-1820.* Scunthorpe: Scunthorpe Museum & Art Gallery, [c.1977?]. Lists landowners from enclosure awards.

Anderby
See Lindsey

Ashby
See Bottesford

Barton on Humber
RUSSELL, REX C. *The enclosures of Barton-upon-Humber, 1793-6, and Hibaldstow, 1796-1803.* Barton upon Humber: Barton Branch, [1962]. Includes list of landowners.
RUSSELL, REX CHARLES. *The enclosure of Barton upon Humber, 1793-6.* Barton upon Humber: Workers Educational Association Barton Branch, 1968. Much revised version of 1962 volume; lists proprietors.

Bottesford
RUSSELL, REX C. *The enclosures of Bottesford & Yaddlethorpe, 1794-7, Messingham, 1798-1804, and Ashby, 1801-1809.* Journal of the Scunthorpe Museum Society **1**, 1964. Includes lists of proprietors.

Burton on Stather
RUSSELL, REX C. *The enclosures of Burton upon Stather, Thealby and Coleby, 1803-1806; Winterton, 1770-1772.* Journal of the Scunthorpe Museum Society, series 1, **2**, 1970. Includes list of landowners from the awards.

Caistor
See Searby

Coleby
See Burton on Stather

East Halton

RUSSELL, REX C. *The enclosures of East Halton, 1801-1804 & North Kelsey, 1813-1840.* Barton upon Humber: Workers Educational Association, 1964. Lists landowners from the enclosure awards.

East Holland

Lincolnshire. East and West Fens Division. An alphabetical list of claims of the proprietors of houses, toftsteads and lands in the East Holland towns having right of common on the said Fens, with a description of the estates ... Boston: Hellaby, 1807. List made prior to enclosure.

Grimsby

See Scartho

Hibaldstow

See Barton on Humber and Scawby

Holbeach

Lincolnshire: Holbeach & Whaplode enclosure: an alphabetical list of claims of lords of manors and of the proprietors of messuages, cottages, toftsteads and lands in the parishes of Holbeach and Whaplode ... Spalding: T. Albin, 1812.

Holton le Clay

RUSSELL, REX C. *The enclosures of Holton le Clay, Waltham and Tetney, 1769-1771.* Barton on Humber: Workers Educational Association Waltham Branch, 1972. Includes list of landowners from the award, 1766.

Horncastle

RUSSELL, ELEANOR, & RUSSELL, REX C. *Old and new landscapes in the Horncastle area.* Lincoln: Lincolnshire County Council Recreational Services, Libraries, 1985.

Kesteven

MILLS, DENNIS R. 'Enclosure in Kesteven', *Agricultural history review* **7**, 1959, 82-97.

Kirton in Lindsey

See Scawby

Lindsey

RUSSELL, ELEANOR, & RUSSELL, REX. *Making new landscapes in Lincolnshire: the enclosures of thirty four parishes.* Lincolnshire history series 5. Lincoln: Lincolnshire Recreational Services, 1983. In mid-Lindsey, gives names of landowners from enclosure awards.

SWALES, T.H. 'The Parliamentary enclosures of Lindsey', *A.A.S.R.P.* **42**(2), 1937, 233-74. Includes list of proprietors for Anderby Outmarsh.

SWALES, T.H. *The Parliamentary enclosures of Lindsey, II*, *L.A.A.S.R.P.* N.S. **1**, 1939, 85-120. Includes list of enclosure commissioners.

Market Rasen

RUSSELL, R.C. *The enclosures of Market Rasen, 1779-1781, and of Wrawby cum Brigg, 1800-1805.* [Market Rasen]: [ ], 1969. Includes list of landowners from the award.

Messingham

See Bottesford

Nettleton

See Searby

North Kelsey

See East Halton

North Thoresby

RUSSELL, REX C. *Revolution in North Thoresby, Lincolnshire: the enclosure of the parish by Act of Parliament, 1836-1846.* [North Thoresby]: North Thoresby Workers Educational Association, 1976. Includes list of landowners.

Scartho

GILLETT, E.E., RUSSELL, REX C., & TREVITT, E.H. *The enclosures of Scartho and Grimsby, 1827-1840.* Grimsby: Libraries & Museum Committee, 1964. Includes lists of landowners.

Scawby

RUSSELL, REX C. *The enclosures of Scawby, 1770-1771, Kirton in Lindsey, 1793-1801, and of Hibaldstow, 1796-1801 & Hibaldstow, 1796-1803.* Workers Educational Association Barton on Humber Branch, 1970. Includes list of landowners from the awards.

Scotter
See Alkborough

Scotterthorpe
See Alkborough

Searby
RUSSELL, R.C. *The enclosures of Searby, 1763-1765; Nettleton, 1791-1795; Caistor, 1796-1798 and Caistor Moors, 1811-1814.* New ed. Caistor: Workers Educational Association (Nettleton Branch), 1968.

South Humberside
RUSSELL, ELEANOR, & RUSSELL, REX C. *Landscape changes in South Humberside: the enclosures of thirty-seven parishes.* Hull: Humberside Leisure Services, 1982. Includes names of landowners from enclosure awards.

Tetney
See Holton le Clay

Thealby
See Burton on Stather

West Halton
See Alkborough

Whaplode
See Holbeach

Whitton
See Alkborough

Winterton
See Burton on Stather

Yaddlethorpe
See Bottesford

17. EDUCATIONAL RECORDS

The records of schools can provide the genealogist with much information on teachers, students, and others associated with them. A number of school histories have been published. These usually list headmasters; they may also mention other staff, pupils, governors, etc. Some, of course, are much more useful to genealogists than others. The list which follows is not comprehensive; rather, it aims to identify those histories which may be of interest to genealogists.

Alford
M[ADDISON], A.R. '[List of boys admitted to Alford Grammar School, 1660-86]', *L.N.Q.* 11, 1911, 6-16. See also 48-9, & 13, 1914, 181-3.

Ashby de la Launde
See Elsham Hall

Elsham Hall
GIBBONS, G.S. 'List of girls at Mrs Gardener's School, 1811 and 1815-20', *L.N.Q.* 18, 1925, 6-9. See also 48. Reprinted in *L.F.H.S.M.* 2(4), 1991, 147-8. Lists 89 pupils of schools at Elsham Hall and Ashby de la Launde.

Heighington
'Names and homes of scholars attending Heighington Grammar School on May 15th, 1777 ...', *L.N.Q.* 16, 1921, 180-81.

Horncastle
CLARKE, J.N. *Education in a market town: Horncastle, Lincolnshire.* Chichester: Phillimore & Co., 1976. Extensive general study, with useful list of sources.
FINDELL, P.W. *Four hundred years of the history of Queen Elizabeth's Grammar School, Horncastle, its governors, its staff, its pupils and its buildings.* Louth: Allinson and Wilcox, 1571. Includes lists of headmasters, 1613-1962, and governors, 1571-1853; also rental 1662, listing tenants.
JALLAND, R. *The free grammar school of Queen Elizabeth in Horncastle, with a current history of the charity from 1599 to 1894 ... a transcript of the school register, and a few personal recollections of the school fifty years ago.* Horncastle: W.K. Morton, 1894.

Lincoln

GARTON, CHARLES. *Schola Lincolniensis: Lincoln School (since 1974 the Lincoln Christs Hospital School): a summary honours board.* 2nd ed. Lincoln: the Old Christ's Hospital Lincolnians Society, 1994. Gives many names of former pupils.

Louth

GOULDING, RICHARD W. *Some Louth Grammar School boys of the XVIth and XVIIth centuries.* 8 pts. [Louth: Goulding,] 1925-32.
WARE, ANDREW. *Louth Grammar School: a history.* Haddington: Charles Skilton, 1989. Includes biographical notes on 'celebrated scholars'.

Osgodby

WILKINSON, ALAN, & WEST, ROSEMARY. *Osgodby School, 1868-1923.* Edinburgh: Pentland Press, 1984. Includes reconstruction of the register, 1869 and 1871, list of teachers, 1869-1924, *etc.*

Stamford

DEED, B.L. *A history of Stamford School.* [Stamford]: Stamford School, 1954. Includes list of rectors of Stamford St.Paul, list of old Stamfordians known to have been at Cambridge, 1532-1912, list of headmasters, 1907-53, roll of honour, 1899-1945, *etc.*

Wrangle

WEST, F. 'The charity school in Wrangle', *L.H.* 2(10), 1963, 1-13. Names some schoolmasters.

Students from Lincoln who attended Cambridge University are listed in:
GARTON, CHARLES. 'The Cambridge connection of old Lincolnshire schools: a checklist', *History of Education Society bulletin* **20,** 1977, 3-27.

Lincolnshire student teachers who attended the Methodist Training College, 1844-71, are listed in:
LEACH, TERENCE. 'Methodist ancestors: some sources, part 1', *S.L.H.A.F.H.S.N.* **5,** 1975, 4-7; **6,** 1980, 6-7.

18. MIGRATION

The descendants of Lincolnshire men may be found in many parts of the world. In order to trace emigrants, you need access to records both in England, and in the places where they settled. There are a number of substantial works listing Lincolnshire migrants; they are mainly concerned with transported convicts. See:
'Lincolnshire' in: COLDHAM, PETER WILSON. *Bonded passengers to America, volume IX: Midland Circuit, 1671-1775 . . .* Baltimore: Genealogical Publishing Co., 1983, 12-19.
ANDERSON, C.L. *Lincolnshire convicts to Australia, Bermuda and Gibraltar: a study of two thousand convicts.* Lincoln: Leace Books, 1993. Includes lists of transportees to Australia, 1787-1868, to Bermuda, mid-19th c., and to Gibraltar, mid-19th c.
ANDERSON, C.L. *Lincolnshire links with Australia, 1788-1840.* Gainsborough: G.W. Belton, 1988. Includes list of transportees, 1787-1840.
ANDERSON, C.L. *Convicts of Lincolnshire.* [Lincoln]: Lincolnshire County Council, 1988. Lists convicts transported to Australia, 1789-1840.
BURNS, CHRIS J. *Colonial round-up, volume one: a directory of Lincolnshire born emigrants who married in the state of Victoria, Australia, 1866-1913.* [ ]: L.F.H.S., 1990.

Family Name Index

Place Name Index

Lincolnshire *continued*

Overseas

Author Index

Dall, C.H. 40
Dalton, C. 41
Darby, H.C. 10
Davey, P. 20
Davies, S. 75
Davis, F.N. 71
Davis, S.N. 18
Dawber, E. 20
Deacon, E. 27, 61
Dear, J. 7
Deed, B.L. 92
Deedes, G.F. 46
Dennis, F. 38
Desforges, A.N. 27
Dewar, P.B. 23
Dickins, B. 30
Dimock, J.F. 71
Dixon, W. 19
Dodds, J.O. 29
Dodds, M.H. 8
Dodds, R. 8
Dods, H. 18
Dolphin, T.W. 44, 50
Dove, J. 39
Dover, P. 9
Dudding, R.C. 10, 26, 32,
  33, 42-52, 57, 73, 77-81,
  84-88
Dunn, C.J. 8
Dyson, A.G. 69

Eagle, E.C. 19
East, F.W. 85
Elder, E. 35
Elliott, S. 11
Ellis, R. 20
Elvin, L. 19, 39, 73
Elwes, D.G.C. 27
Eminson, T.B.F. 65
Emptage, E. 68
Engelbach, G.F. 48
Evans, C. 39
Everson, P.L. 8
Evison, J. 28
Exley, C.L. 86

F., F.R. 80
F., W.E. 15, 26
Fane, W.K. 21
Farmery, E. 23
Farrer, W. 76
Fawcett, R. 46

Finch, M. 13
Fincham, H.W. 83
Findell, P.W. 91
Fiske, J.F. 40
Fletcher, A. 10
Fletcher, W.G.D. 25, 28, 34,
  61, 89
Foljambe, C.G.S. 27
Footman, M.H. 11, 88
Foottit, E.H. 51
Fordham, P. 84
Foster, C.W. 23, 25, 35,
  43-45, 48, 58, 59, 66, 71,
  72, 81, 83, 84
Foster, W.E. 28, 31, 34, 57,
  61, 62, 72, 74, 82
Fowler, J.T. 28, 53
Franklin, P. 33
Friedrichs, R.L. 60
Fuller, J.F. 35

G., A.H. 25
G., S.G. 62
Gainsford, W.D. 29
Galbraith, V.H. 83
Gant, F. 45
Garford, J. 29
Garner, A.A. 9, 29
Garton, C. 32, 92
Gaskell, E. 17
Gates, L.C. 21
Gerald of Wales 71
Gerlis, D. 75
Gerlis, L. 75
Gibbons, A. 16, 29, 42, 59,
  72, 78, 80, 82
Gibbons, G.S. 19, 58, 91
Gillett, E. 10, 20, 79, 90
Gillow, J. 44
Goff, C. 24
Good, J. 66
Goodricke, C.A. 29
Gordon, R. 15
Goshawk, P. 66
Gough, R. 83
Goulding, R.W. 20, 22, 30,
  46, 55, 74, 80, 83, 85, 87,
  92
Graves, C.V. 69
Green, E. 16, 22-25, 27-29,
  31, 35, 38-41, 75
Green, P.L.L. 44

Greenfield, B.W. 24
Greenfield, L. 79
Greenhill, F.A. 53
Greenstreet, J. 66
Greenway, D.E. 72
Greenwood, I.J. 24
Griffin, J.A.A. 21
Grigg, D. 8, 67
Gunn, S.J. 8
Gurnhill, J. 45

H., J.C. 61
Hains, G. 59
Hall, A. 11
Hall, J.G. 7
Hall, T.W. 82
Hallam, H.E. 8, 84, 86
Hallett, G.C. 20
Hamilton, F. 44
Handley, R.C. 30
Hansom, J.S. 32
Hanson, P.H. 18
Harding, A. 76
Harding, L. 43, 46, 51
Harding, N.S. 70
Hardy, W.J. 82
Harris, H.R. 53
Harris, J. 7
Hartley, J.S. 80, 86
Hawkesbury, Lord 57
Hay, K. 12
Heanley, R.M. 60
Hemingway, G. 25, 30
Heron, V. 20
Hett, M.J.F. 30
Hewson, T. 30
Higgins, A. 28
Higgins, C.A. 22
Hill, F., Sir 9, 11
Hill, J.W.F. 11, 23, 32, 71,
  80, 82, 86
Hill, R. 69, 71
Hinton, R.W.K. 20
Historical Manuscripts
  Commission 70, 78, 79
Hoare, D. 74
Hodgett, G.A.J. 7, 71
Holderness, B.A. 8, 9, 21, 33
Holland, P. 8
Holles, G. 31, 52, 54, 56
Holmes, C. 7, 10
Holtzmann, W. 71

105

Hooper, L. 11
Hooson, P.L. 51
Hosford, W.H. 85, 86, 89
Hoskins, J.P. 74
Hostettler, E. 12
Howard, W.F. 50
Howlett, E. 79
Huddleston, G. 31
Hudson, J.C. 47
Hulme, H. 38
Humberside Libraries 12
Hunnisett, R.F. 76
Hunt, A. 17, 37
Hunt, R.W. 72
Hunter, A.W.H. 31
Hutton, A.W. 31

Imray, J. 24
Ingham, M.J. 17
Irby, P.A. 31

Jackson, C. 10, 35, 85
Jackson, G. 25
Jalland, R. 91
James, M.E. 8
Jarvis, E.G. 86
Jeans, G.E. 53, 56, 57
Jefferson, J.K. 12
Jensen, G.F. 7, 83
Jessopp, A. 39
Jeudwine, G.W. 44, 46
Johnson, C.P.C. 42, 45, 48, 82
Johnson, R.W. 31
Johnston, J.A. 19, 59
Jones, E.D. 84
Jones, S. 20, 88

Kennedy, M.E. 10, 77
Kennedy, P.A. 34
Kent, P.R. 61
Kershaw, B.R. 58
Ketchell, C. 12
Ketteringham, J. 17, 70, 73
Ketteringham, S. 22
Kimball, E.G. 76
King, E. 39
King, H.P.F. 72
King, R.D. 50
King-Fane, W. 75, 76
Kirk, R.E.G. 32
Kirkus, A.M. 77

Knight, F. 70
Knox, M. 33

L., B.L. 85
L., L.B. 83
Lamming, D. 18
Lang, C.H.D. 27
Langley, A.S. 74
Langley, C.E. 39
Langton, C. 32
Larken, A.S. 15, 24
Layton, W.E. 35
Le Neve, J. 72
Leach, T. 38, 75, 87, 88, 92
Leadam, I.S. 76
Leary, W. 36, 74, 75
Lee, A. 21
Leighton-Boyce, J.A.S.L. 37
Lewin, S. 52
Lewis, A.S. 36
Lewis, F.C. 86
Lincoln, Precentor of 55
Lincolnshire Archives
   Committee 13
Lincolnshire Archives
   Office 42, 77
Lindley, K. 10
Linnell, R.J. 19
Livesey, J. 32
Livesey, R. 33
Lodge, S. 33
Longley, T. 32, 39, 66
Lord, J. 53
Lowe, F.P. 83
Lyons, N. 89

M., H. 63
M., J. 55
M., S.S.C.J. 27, 29
Macdonald, G.W. 46, 79
Mackinder, A. 17, 18, 77, 80
Macray, W.D. 79
Maddison, A.R. 8, 15, 16, 22, 24-34, 36-38, 44, 48, 49, 53-62, 70, 73, 77, 78, 85-88, 91
Maddison, P. 34
Major, K. 27, 69, 70, 72, 73, 82, 88
Maples, A.K. 44, 45, 48-51
Marrat, W. 7, 78
Marriott, G.L. 35

Marsh, B. 18
Marshall, G.W. 37
Maser, F.E. 39
Massingberd, W.O. 23, 26, 30, 32-34, 37-39, 41, 50, 63, 67, 72, 74, 81, 83, 84, 85-89
Mathews, W.A. 43
May, A. 33
Mayr-Harting, H. 69
McHardy, A.K. 67, 69
McIntyre, I. 45
McLane, B. 8, 76
Mellows, W.T. 83
Metcalfe, W.C. 15
Middlebrook, M. 75
Miller, K. 7
Miller, V. 43-48, 50, 51
Mills, D.R. 7, 8, 19, 67, 90
Mills, J. 67
Minet, W. 74
Monson, J., Lord 52
Moore, M.P. 25
Moore, W. 17
Morgan, F.W. 37
Morgan, P. 37, 66
Moriarty, G.A. 24, 61
Morris, C. 69
Morris, L.J. 31
Morton, W. 29
Mowbray, D. 43
Myddleton, W.M. 27

Nannestad, D. 18
Nannestad, E. 11, 12
Nannestad, I. 18
Neave, D. 20, 60
Neill, E. 79
Neill, N. 40
Neilson, N. 85
Neller, R. 12
Nevill, E.R. 34
Nichols, J. 81
Nichols, J.G. 8, 32
Nicholson, S.W. 35
Noble, J. 65
Norgate, K. 11, 88
North, T. 70
Nottingham, Bishop of 58

Obelkevich, J. 9
Oliver, J.W. 60
Olney, R.J. 7, 9

106

107